WHEN I WAS A BOY IN JAPAN

塩谷栄

SHIO・YA・SAKAE

Sakae Shioya

WHEN I WAS A BOY IN JAPAN

BY

SAKAE SHIOYA

ILLUSTRATED FROM PHOTOGRAPHS

Zea Books
Lincoln, Nebraska
2022

Published & copyright 1906 by Lothrop, Lee & Shepard Co.

ISBN 978-1-60962-246-6 paperback
ISBN 978-1-60962-247-3 ebook
doi: 10.32873/unl.dc.zea.1324

Zea Books are published by the
University of Nebraska-Lincoln Libraries.

Electronic (pdf) edition available online at
https://digitalcommons.unl.edu/zeabook/

Print edition available from Lulu.com at
http://www.lulu.com/spotlight/unllib

University of Nebraska-Lincoln does not discriminate
based upon any protected status. Please go to
http://www.unl.edu/equity/notice-nondiscrimination

PREFACE

JAPANESE boys have not been introduced very much to their little American friends, and the purpose of this book is to provide an introduction by telling some of the experiences which are common to most Japanese boys of the present time, together with some account of the customs and manners belonging to their life. I can at least claim that the story is told as it could be only by one who had actually lived the life that is portrayed. I have endeavored to hold the interest of my young readers by bringing in more or less of amusement. The little girl companion is introduced to widen the interest and add somewhat more of the story element than would otherwise be present. The sketches composing the various chapters are necessarily disconnected, but they form a series of pictures, priceless at least to the author, which foreign eyes have seldom been allowed to see.

SAKAE SHIOYA.

YALE UNIVERSITY, 1905.

CONTENTS

CHAPTER I. : My Infancy.
How I Looked. — My Name — Walking — In Tea Season — My Toys — "Kidnapped" — O-dango 11

CHAPTER II. : At Home.
Introduction — Dinner — Rice — Turning to Cows – A Bamboo Dragon-fly — A Watermelon Lantern — On a Rainy Evening — The Story of a Badger 20

CHAPTER III. : The Village School.
A Mimic School — Preparations — The School — How Classes Are Conducted — Out of Tune — A Moral Story — School Discipline — Playthings — "Knife Sense" 27

CHAPTER IV. : In Tokyo.
Where We Settled — A Police Stand — Stores — "Broadway" — Illumination — The Foreign Settlement 37

CHAPTER V. : My New School.
Tomo-chan — The Men with Wens — A Curious Punishment – How I Experienced It — Kotoro-Kotoro 45

CONTENTS.

CHAPTER VI. : CHINESE EDUCATION.
My Chinese Teacher — How I Was Taught — Versification — My Uncle — Clam Fishing — A Flatfish 53

CHAPTER VII. : AN EVENING FÊTE.
My Father — His Love for Potted Trees — A Local Fête — Show Booths — Goldfish Booths — Singing Insects — How a Potted Tree Was Bought 63

CHAPTER VIII. : SUMMER DAYS.
A Swimming School — How I Was Taught to Swim — Diving — The Old Home Week — Return of the Departed Souls — Visiting the Ancestral Graves — The Memorable Night — A Village Dance 70

CHAPTER IX. : THE ENGLISH SCHOOL.
A Night at the Dormitory — Beginning English — Grammar — Pronunciation — School Moved — Mother's Love 77

CHAPTER X. : A BOY ASTRONOMER.
What I Intended to Be — My Aunt's View — My Parents' Approval — My Uncle's Enthusiasm — The Total Eclipse of the Sun 86

CHAPTER XI.: IN THE SUBURBS.
A Novel Experiment — Removal — Our New House — Angling — Tomo-chan's Visit 95

ILLUSTRATIONS

PAGE

SAKAE SHIOYA	*Portrait Frontispiece*
A JAPANESE HOUSE.	19
A JAPANESE SCHOOL SCENE	31
THE JAPANESE "BROADWAY"	40
A TYPICAL JAPANESE STREET	61
A JAPANESE SCHOOL OF THE PRESENT DAY	80

WHEN I WAS A BOY IN JAPAN

CHAPTER I

MY INFANCY

How I Looked — My Name — Walking — In Tea Season — My Toys — "Kidnapped" — O-dango.

I suppose I don't need to tell you exactly, my little friends, when and where I was born, because Japanese names are rather hard for you to remember, and then I don't want to disclose my age. Suffice it to say that I was once a baby like all of you and my birthplace was about a day's journey from Tokyo, the capital of Japan. I wish I could have observed myself and noted down every funny thing I did when very small, as the guardian angel, who is said to be standing by every cradle, will surely do. But when my memory began to be serviceable, I was well on in my infancy, and if I were to rely on that only, I should have to skip over a considerable length of time. How I should dislike to do this! So, my little friends, let me construct this chapter out of bits of things my mamma used to tell me now and then.

When I was born, my father was away. Grandma was very proud to have a boy for the first-born, and at once wrote him a letter saying that a son was born to him and that he was like — and then she wrote two large circles, meaning that I was very, very plump. Do you know how a plump Japanese baby looks? I have often wondered myself, and have many a time watched a baby taking a bath. Let us suppose him to be one year old and about to be put into warm water in a wooden tub. His chin is dimple-cleft, his cheeks ripe as an apple, and his limbs are but a continuation of his fat trunk. And how jolly the elfin is! After the queer expression he has shown on being dipped has passed away and he realizes what he is about, he will make many quick bows — really, I assure you, to show his thanks for the trouble of washing him. At this, mother, sister, and the maid assisting them give a burst of laughter, when, with a scream of immense delight, he will strike his fists into the water, causing a panic among the well-clad and not-ready-to-get-wet attendants. With royal indifference, however, he will then try to push his fist into his mouth, and not grumbling at all over his ill-success, he will set about telling a story with his everlasting mum-mum. Now he is taken out and laid on a towel. Glowing red, how he will move his arms and legs like an overturned turtle! Well, that is how I looked, I am very sure.

In Japan, in christening a child, we follow the principle of "A good name is better than rich ointment." I was named Sakae, which in the hierographic Chinese characters represents fire burning on a stand. The idea of illumination will perhaps suggest itself to you

MY INFANCY

at once, and indeed, it means glory or thrift. And my well-wishing parents named me so, that I might thrive and be a glory to my family. So I was bound to be good, wasn't I? A bad boy with a good name would be very much like a monkey with a silk hat on.

Now begins my walking. Now and then mamma or grandma would train me, taking my hands and singing:

> "Anyo wa o-jozu,
> Korobu wa o-heta."

But my secret delight — so I judge — was to stand by myself, clinging to the convenient checkered frames of paper screens, which covered the whole length of the veranda. When I went from one side to the other, at first without being noticed — of course walking like a crab — and then suddenly being discovered with a shout of admiration, I used to come down with a bump, which, however, never hurt me — I was so plump, you know. I must describe here a sort of ceremony, or rather an ordeal, I had to pass through when I was fairly able to stand and walk without any help. For this I must begin with my house.

My house stood on the outskirts of the town, where the land rose to a low hill and was covered with tea-plants. We owned a part of it hedged in by criptomerias.

We were not regular tea dealers, but we used to have an exciting time in the season preparing our crop. Lots of red-cheeked country girls would come to pick the leaves, and it was a sight to see them working. With their heads nicely wrapped with pieces of white and blue cloth, jetting out of the green ocean of tea-leaves, they would sing peculiarly effective country songs, mostly in solos with a short refrain in chorus. But they were not having a concert, and if you should step in among them, they would make a hero of you, those girls. And then we had also a good many young men working at tea-heaters.

Here they likewise sang snatches of songs, but their principal business was to roll up steamed leaves and dry them over the fire. But when work is combined with fun, it is a great temptation for a boy, and I, a lad of five or six, I remember, would have a share among them, and, standing on a high stool by a heater and baring my right shoulder like the rest, would join more in a refrain than in rolling the leaves.

But I was going to tell you about the ceremony I had to pass through, wasn't I? Well, it happened, or rather somebody especially arranged it so, I suspect, that I should have it just at the time of this great excitement. The ceremony itself is like this. They take a child fairly able to walk, load him with some heavy thing, and place him in a sort of a large basket shaped like the blade of a shovel. Now let him walk. The basket will rock under him, the load is too heavy for him, and he will fall down.

If he does, it is taken for granted that he has in that one act had all the falls that he would otherwise meet in his later life. So, if he appears too strong to stumble, he will be shaken down by some roguish hands before he gets out of it.

I was to go through this before august spectators — country girls. They liked to see me plump, because some of them were even more plump than I. At any rate, from everywhere they saluted me as "Bot'chan," "Bot'chan." If I had returned every salute by looking this way and that, I should have broken my neck. But it was customary to make a bow anyway, and I was ordered by my mamma to do so. On this occasion I made two snap bows with my chin, which excited laughter. Now a basket was produced, a brand-new one, I remember, and I was loaded with some heavy rice cake. I stood up, however, like Master Peachling of our fairy-tale, who is said to have surprised his adopted mother by rising in his bathtub on the very day of his birth! I was then placed in the basket and made to walk.

I looked intently at the basket, not because it was new, but because it gave me a queer motion, the ups and downs of a boat, a new sensation to me, anyway. Attracted, however, by the merry voices of the crowd, I looked at them, and suddenly, being pleased with so many smiling faces, raised a cry of delight, when down I came with a loud noise. A roar of laughter broke out with the clapping of hands. The noise buried my surprise and I also clapped my hands without knowing who was being cheered.

As the first-born of the house, I must have had lots of playthings. But there were two things I remember as clear as the day. One was a sword, all wood, however. As the son of a samurai, I should have had to serve my lord under the old régime and stake my life and honor on the two blades of steel. And so even if the good old days were gone, something to remind us of them was kept and made a plaything of. But really, I liked my wooden sword. The other thing was a horse — a hobby-horse, I mean. I don't know just how many horses I had, but I wanted any number of them. I had some pictures, but they were all of horses. If not, I would not accept the presents. And with these two kinds of treasures I enjoyed most of my childhood days, the sword slantingly on my side, and the horse, which I fancied trotting, under me, while I shouted "Haiyo! haiyo!"

Although I had my own name, people called me "Bot'chan," as I have said, be cause it is a general term of endearment, and papa and mamma would call me "Bô" or "Bôya." Among those who addressed me thus, I remember very well one middle-aged woman who often came to steal me from mamma, and by whom I was only too glad to be stolen.

We had a long veranda facing the garden, on which I passed most of my days. There I rode on my hobby-horse or played with my little dog Shiro, who would go through all sorts of tricks for a morsel of nice things. Suddenly my laugh would cease and nothing of me would be heard. Wondering what the matter was, mamma would open the paper screen to see, and lo! not a shadow of me was to be seen. Even Shiro had disappeared. Attacked with a feeling something akin to horror, she used to picture — so I imagine — a winged tengu (a Japanese harpy) swooping down and carrying me away to some distant hill. But soon finding recent steps of clogs on the ground, coming to and receding from the veranda, she would nod and smile at the trick. She knew that I had been kidnapped by a good soul!

Now I want to give you some reasons why I liked this woman. First of all, it was because she always carried me on her back. The only way to appreciate what it is to be tall, would be to be a grown-up man and a small child at the same time. And that is exactly the feeling that I had. I could see lots of curious things over the forbidden hedges. I could even see things over the house-tops; they were all one-story, and built low, though. In a word, I always felt while on her back like a wee pig who had first toddled out into a wide, wide world. And then she would carry me through town. What life there was! After crossing a bridge which spanned the stream, coming from the beautiful lake on the north and going a little way along a row of pine-trees, we would come on a flock of ducks and geese on their way to the water. What a noise they made, — quack, quack! Then we would begin inspecting rows of houses, open to the street and in which all sorts of things were sold. Men, women, and children, as well as dogs, seemed to be very much occupied. Then I would spy some horses laden with straw bags and wood. Real horses they were, but I was rather disappointed to find them so big and their appearance not half so good as in my pictures. My faith in them always began to shake a little bit, but still I used to persist in thinking that my hobby horses and pictures were nearer the reality than those we met on the street. And wasn't it curious that my belief was at last substantiated by seeing a Shetland pony in America after some twenty years? Ah, that was exactly what I had in mind!

Then I would hear a merry prattle on a drum — *terent-tenten, terent-tenten*. Ah, here would come boy acrobats dressed in something like girls' gymnasium suits, with a small mask of a lion's head with a plume on it, on their heads. A funny sort of boy, I thought, but on my woman's giving them some pennies, they would perform all sorts of feats which interested me never so much. The woman used to shake me to make sure that I was not dead, as I kept very quiet, watching.

The woman's house was just behind the street, and she was sure to take me there. Here was another reason why I liked her very much. She seemed to know just what I wanted. She would set me on the sunny veranda and bring me some nice o-dango (rice dumpling). This she made herself, and it was prepared just to my liking, covered well with soy and baked deliciously. I was in clover if I only had that!

I will describe one of my visits, which will well represent them all. The day was calm and bright, and while we were feasting — she had some of the good things, too — her pussy sat on one end of the veranda and was finishing her toilet in the sun. Even the sparrows in this peaceful weather forgot that they were birds of air, and fell from the trees and were wrestling noisily on the ground. Only the pussy's move broke up their sport. By this time we were very near the end of our business. Turning from the sparrows, my woman glanced at me and sat for a moment transfixed with the awful sight I presented. There I was with my cheeks and nose all besmeared with brown soy, stretching my sticky hands in a helpless attitude, and licking my mouth by way of variation. She now broke into laughter and was scrambling on the floor, weak with merriment. But my mute appeal was too eloquent; indeed, I was all ready to shed tears with an utter sense of helplessness when she hastened to bring a wet towel and wipe my face and hands clean and nice, with, "Oh, my poor Bot'chan!"

A Japanese House.

CHAPTER II

AT HOME

Introduction — Dinner — Rice — Turning to Cows —
A Bamboo Dragon-fly — A Watermelon Lantern —
On a Rainy Evening — The Story of a Badger.

OUR family consisted of father, mother, grandmother, and two children besides myself, at the time when I was six years old. I don't remember exactly what business my father was in, but my impression is that he had no particular one. He had been trained for the old samurai and devoted most of his youthful days to fencing, riding, and archery. But by the time he had come of age, that training was of no use to him professionally, because, as quickly as you can turn the palm of your hand, Japan went through a wonderful change from the old feudal régime to the era of new civilization. So my father, and many, many others like him, were just in mid-air, so to speak, being thrown out of their proper sphere, but unable to settle as yet to the solid ground and adapt themselves to new ways. My mother came also of the samurai stock, and, like most of her class, kept in her cabinet a small sword beautifully ornamented in gold work, with which she was ready to defend her honor whenever obliged to. But far from being mannish, she was as meek as a lamb, and was devoted to my father and her children. My grand-

AT HOME.

mother was of a retiring nature and I cannot draw her very much into my narrative. But she was very good to everybody, and her daily work, so far as I can remember, was to take a walk around the farm every morning. She was so regular in this habit that I cannot think of her without associating her with the scent of the dewy morning and with the green of the field which stretched before her. She died not many years after, but I often wonder if she is really dead. To me she is still living, and what the great poet said of Lucy Gray sounds peculiarly true in her case, too.

> " — Yet some maintain that to this day
>   She is a living child;
> That you may see sweet Lucy Gray
>   Upon the lonesome wild.
>
> "O'er rough and smooth she trips along,
>   And never looks behind;
> And sings a solitary song
>   That whistles in the wind."

Only you would have to make Lucy seventy years old to fit my grandmother.

The introduction being over, let us attend a dinner, or rather give attention to a description of one. We do not eat at one large dining-table with chairs around it. We each have a separate small table about a foot and a half square, all lacquered red, green, or black, and sit before it on our heels. A rice bucket, a tea pot, some saucers, a bottle of soy, and so forth, are all placed near some one who is to specially serve us. We used to sit in two rows, father and grandmother facing each

CHAPTER II.

other, mother next to father, with the young sister opposite my brother and myself. The younger children usually sit next to some older person who can help them in eating. No grace was said, but I always bowed to my elders before I began with "itadakimasu " (I take this with thanks), which I sometimes said when I was very hungry, as a good excuse and signal to start eating before the others.

Rice is our staple food and an almost reverential attitude toward it as the sustainer of our life is entertained by the people. And I was told time and again not to waste it. Once a maid, so my mother used to tell me, was very careless in cleaning rice before it was cooked. She dropped lots of grains on the stone floor under the sink day after day, and never stopped to pick them up. One day, when she wanted to clean the floor, she was frightened half to death by finding there ever so many white serpents straining their necks at her. She really fainted when the goddess of the kitchen appeared to her in her trance and bade her to take all those white serpents in a basket and wash them clean. As she came to herself, she did as she was told, trembling with horror at touching such vile things, some of which, indeed, would try to coil themselves around her hands. But as the last pailful of water was poured on them, lo! what were serpents a moment ago were now all turned into nice grains of rice ready to be boiled. Now if there is one thing in the world I hate, it is a serpent; the mere mention of it makes my flesh creep. So you see I took care to pitch every grain of boiled rice into my mouth with my chop-sticks before I left my table.

AT HOME.

Another story was told me concerning the meal. The Japanese teach home discipline by stories, you know. This was a short one, being merely the statement that if anybody lies down on the floor soon after he has eaten his meal, he will turn into a cow. Now a number of times I had found cows chewing their cuds while stretched upon the ground. So I thought, in my childish mind, that there must be some mysterious connection between each of the three in the order as they stand: eating — lying down — cow. So, naturally, I avoided the second process, and, after eating, immediately ran out-of-doors to see what our man, Kichi, was doing.

Kichi worked on our little farm, and I usually found him cleaning his implements after the day's work. We were great friends, and he used to present me with toys of his own making, which were very simple but indeed a marvel to me. Once he picked up a piece of bamboo and made a chip of it about a twelfth of an inch thick, a third of an inch wide, and three inches and a half long. Then he sliced obliquely one-half of one side and the other half of the same side in the opposite direction, so that the edges might be made thin. He also bored a small hole in the middle and put in a stick about twice as thick as a hairpin and about four inches long, the sliced side being down. He then cut off the projecting end of the stick, when it was tight in the chip. The dragon-fly was now ready to take flight. He took the stick between his palms and gave a twist, when lo! it flew away up in the air.

I was delighted with the toy, and tried several times to make it fly. But when I used all my force and gave it a good long twist, why, it took such a successful flight that it hit the edge of the comb of our straw roof and stuck there, never to come down. I was very sorry at that, but Kichi laughed at the feat the dragon-fly had performed, and said that the maker was so skilful that the toy turned out to be a real living thing! It was perched there for the night. Well, I admired his skill very much, but did not want to lose my toy in that way. So I made him promise me to make another the next day, reminding him not to put too much skill in it.

It was summer, the season of watermelons. We had a small melon patch and an ample supply of the fruit. Here was a chance for Kichi to try his skill again. One evening he took a pretty round melon and scooped the inside out so as to put in a lighted candle. So far this was very ordinary. He scraped the inner part until the rind was fairly transparent, and then cut a mouth, a nose, and eyes with eye brows sticking out like pins. He then painted them so that when the candle was lighted a monster of a melon was produced. How triumphant a boy would feel in possessing such a thing! I hung it on the veranda that evening when the room was weirdly lighted by one or two greenish paper lanterns, and watched it with my folks. I expressed my admiration for Kichi's skill, and with boyish fondness for exaggeration mentioned the fact that a toy dragon-fly of his making had really turned out to be a living thing. All laughed, but of course I made an effort to be serious. But no sooner were we silent than, without the slightest hint, the melon angrily dropped down with a crash. I screamed, but, being assured of its safety, I approached it and found the skull of the monster was badly fractured, in fact, one piece of it flying some twenty feet out in the garden. The next morning I took the first opportunity to tell Kichi that his toy was so skilfully made that it sought death of its own accord.

Well, I started to tell what I did evenings, but when it was wet I had a very tedious time. Nothing is more dismal to a boy than a rainy day. To lie down was to become a cow. So one rainy evening I opened the screen, and, standing, looked out at the rain. But this was no fun. The only alternative was to go to one of the rooms. Now there is no chair in a Japanese house, and to sit over one's heels is too ceremonial, not to say a bit trying, even for a Japanese child. So my legs unconsciously collapsed, and there I was lying on my back, singing aloud some songs I had learned. Presently I began to look at the unpainted ceiling, and traced the grain. And is it not wonderful that out of knots and veins of wood you can make figures of some living things? Yes, I traced a man's face, one eye much larger than the other. Then, I had a cat. Now I began to trace a big one with a V-shaped face. A cow! The idea ran through me with the swiftness of lightning, and the next moment I sprang to my feet and shook myself to see if I had undergone any transformation. Luckily, I was all right. But to make the thing sure, I felt of my forehead carefully to see if any thing hard was coming out of it. The room now lost its attraction. And I ran away to the room where my grandmother was. Opening the screen, I said:

"Grandma!"

"Well, Bô?"

"May I come in? I want you to tell me the story of a badger, grandma."

I was never tired of hearing the same stories over and over again from my grandmother. There was at some distance a tall tree, shooting up like an arrow to the sky, which was visible from a window of her room. It was there that the badger of her story liked to climb. One early evening he was there with the cover of an iron pot, which he made with his magic power appear like a misty moon. Now a farmer, who was still working in the field, chanced to see it, and was surprised to find that it was already so late. He could tell the hour from the position of the moon, you know. So he made haste to finish his work, and was going home, when another moon, the real one this time, peeped out of the wood near by. The badger, however, had too much faith in his art to withdraw his mock moon, and held it there to rival the newly risen one. The farmer was astonished to find two moons at the same time, but he was not slow to see which was real. He smiled at the trick of the badger, and now wanted to outwit him. He approached the tree stealthily and shook it with all his might. The badger was not prepared for this. Losing his balance, he dropped down to the ground, moon and all, and had to run for his life, for the farmer was right after him with his hoe.

I laughed and grandma laughed, too, over her own story, when the paper screen was suddenly brightened.

"The badger's moon!" I cried, and climbed up to my grandmother.

"Yes, I am a badger," said a voice, as the door was opened. And there stood my mother with a paper lantern she had brought for the room.

CHAPTER III

THE VILLAGE SCHOOL

A Mimic School — Preparations — The School — How Classes Are Conducted — Out of Tune — A Moral Story — School Discipline — Playthings — "Knife Sense."

At the age of six I was sent to school. For some time before the fall opening, I was filled with excitement and curiosity and looked forward to the day with great impatience. As our neighbors were few and scattered and I did not have many playmates, I wondered how I should feel on coming in contact with so many boys, most of whom were older than I. And then there was study. I had a faint idea what a learned scholar such as Confucius was, and felt as if a plunge into school a day or two would half convert me into that obscure ideal. Weeks before, I insisted on having a mimic school at home to prepare myself a little for the august event, and with my mother as teacher I learned the numerals and the forty-eight letters of the Japanese alphabet by heart. I wished to do just as I would at school, and so I used to go outdoors and with measured steps approach the porch. Entering the house, I sat down before a table and bowed reverentially. When my mother was there before me, I cheerfully began to study, well, for five minutes or so, but when I found her not quite ready I was mercilessly thrown out of humor, and only her exaggerated bows for apology would induce me to dry my sorrowful tears.

The few days before the opening of the school were taken for my preparation. I needed copy-books, a slate, an abacus, which is a frame strung with wires on which are wooden beads to be moved in counting and reckoning, and a small writing-box, containing a stone ink-well, a cake of India ink, a china water-vessel, and brushes. I must have also a round lunch set, the three pieces of which can be piled one upon another like a miniature pagoda, and then, when empty, be put one within another to reduce the size. A pair of chop-sticks went with the set of course. Now all must be purchased new as if everything had a new start. And then a new school suit was procured together with a navy cap. These were all ready a day before, and were exhibited on the alcove.

My younger brother was possessed of the school mania at the sight of these last, and insisted that he would have his set, too. And so mimic ones were procured, and these formed a second row together with his holiday suit.

And then came the night before I was to go. I played the part of a watch-dog by sleeping right near my property. In fact, I went to bed early, but I could not sleep till after everybody had retired for the night. And then I dreamed that my abacus stood up, its beads chattering on how to start the trip in the morning. It was joined by the copy-book, made of soft, Japanese paper, which parted hither and thither in walking, as a lady's skirt, — a Japanese lady's, I mean. The chairman was my navy cap. I did not know how

THE VILLAGE SCHOOL

they decided, but they must have come to a peaceful agreement, as they were found, when I awoke in the morning, exactly in the same place, lying quiet.

The next morning I set out with my father for the school. The faces of every one in the house were at the door looking at me. I made every effort to be dignified in walking, but could not help looking back just once, when my face relaxed into a smile, and I felt suddenly very shy. But as I heard my younger brother struggling to get away from my mother to follow me, I hastened my steps to turn round a corner of the road.

The school was a low, dark-looking building, with paper-screened windows all around like a broad white belt, and with a spacious porch with dusty shelves to leave clogs on. When we arrived, we were led into a side room, where we met the master or principal, and soon my father returned home, leaving me to his care. I felt somewhat lonesome with strangers all around, but kept myself as cool as possible, which effort was very much like stopping a leak with the hands. A slight neglect would bring something misty into my eyes. But now all the boys — and girls, too, in the other room — came into one large room. Some forty of the older ones and fifteen of those who had newly entered took their seats, the older ones glancing curiously at the newcomers. But we were all in back seats and so were not annoyed with looks that would have been felt piercing us from behind. The desk I was assigned to was a miserable one; not only was it besmeared with ink ages old, but cuts were made here and there as if it were a well-fought battle-ground. But I did not feel ashamed to sit there, as I thought that this was a kind of place in which a Confucius was to be brought up.

Looking awhile on what was going on, I found the boys were divided into three classes. The method of teaching was curious; one class alone was allowed to have a reading lesson, while the other two were having writing or arithmetic, that is, the teaching was so arranged that what one class was doing might not disturb the others. I was struck, even in my boyish mind, with the happy method, and learned the first lesson in management. And then reading was done partly in unison with the master, in a singsong style, and the effect was pleasing, if it was not very loud. The class in arithmetic, on the other hand, sent out a pattering noise of pencils on the slates, which in a confused mass would form an overtone of the orchestra. A writing lesson taken in the midst of such a company was never tiresome. Indeed, anything out of tune would send the whole house into laughter, and such things were constantly happening.

I was not slow in becoming acquainted with the boys. As I went into the playground for the first time, I felt rather awkward to find nobody to play with. But soon two boys whom I knew thrust themselves before me and uncovered their heads. And from that moment the playground became a place of great interest to me. Two friends grew into five, eight, ten, and fifteen, and in three days I felt as if I possessed the whole ground.

As things grew more familiar, I found almost every boy was striving a little bit to be out of tune. When singsong reading was going on, pupils echoing

A Japanese School Scene

responsively the teacher's voice, some wild boy would suddenly redouble his effort with gusto, and his voice, like that of a strangled chicken, would soar away up, to the great merriment of the rest. And then often a boy, whose mind was occupied with a hundred and one things except the book, engaged in some sly communication with another, unconscious of the teacher's approach, when he would literally jump into the air as the master's whip descended sharply on his desk. We sat by twos on benches, and when one boy saw his companion carelessly perching on the end of the bench, just right for experimenting the principle of the lever, he would not miss a moment to stand up, presumably to ask some question. But no sooner had he called to the teacher, than the other fellow would shoot down to the floor with a cry, and the bench come back with a tremendous noise. But this was not all. When the boys could not find a pretense to make a noise, they would stealthily paint their faces with writing brushes. Two touches would be enough to grow a thick mustache curling up to the ears. When the teacher faced a dozen of those mustache-wearing boys who were unable to efface their naughty acts as quickly as they had committed them, he could do nothing but to burst into undignified laughter.

One day a strange method of discipline was instituted. The teacher must have been at a loss to bring the urchins to behave well. It was the last hour, the only hour, I think, the boys kept quiet. They did so partly because the course bore the great name of ethics, but more because moral stories were told. And the boys did not care whether the stories were moral or not, as long as they were interesting. Here is one of the twenty-four Chinese stories that teach filial duty:

> There was once a boy by the name of Ching who had an old mother. He was a good boy, and did what he could to please her. The mother, however, often asked for things hard to get. One day in winter she wanted some carp for her dinner. It was very cold, and the lake where Ching used to fish was all frozen. What could he do? He, however, went to the lake, looked about the place to find out where the ice was not thick, and, baring himself about his stomach, lay flat to thaw it. It was a very difficult thing to do, but at last the ice gave way, and to his great joy, from the crevice thus made, a big carp jumped out into the air. So he could satisfy his mother's want.

Not only the boys who listened intently, but also the teacher, got interested as the story grew to the climax, and the latter would gesticulate and eventually impersonate the dutiful boy, showing surprise at seeing a carp jumping ten feet into the air. This called forth laughter which was meant for applause. But the teacher soon came to himself and called silence. One day, after telling this story, he said that it was yet half an hour before the time to close, but he would dismiss us. "But," he continued, "you can go only one by one, beginning with those who are quiet and good. This is to train you for your orderly conduct in study-hours, and if any one cannot keep quiet, even for half an hour, he shall stay in his place till he can do so." This was a severe test. An early dismissal, even of five minutes before the time, had a special charm for boys, but to-day we could march out half an hour earlier. And then what a lovely day it was in autumn! The warm sun was bright, and the trees were ablaze with golden leaves. Persimmons were waiting for us to climb up and feast on them. After a moment the boys were as still as night. One by one a "good" boy was called to leave; they went like lambs to the door, but no sooner were they out, than some stamped on the stairs noisily and shouted and laughed on the green, which act showed that the teacher did not always pick the right ones. I naturally waited my turn with impatience. I thought I was a pretty good boy. At least I had Confucius for my ideal, and those who had it were not many. I never did mischief, except once, and that was really an accident. I dropped my lunch-box in my arithmetic class, and chased it, as it had rolled off quite a distance. Half the school laughed at me, and that was all. I was now musing on my ill-luck when a call came to me at last. It was still a quarter of an hour before closing time, and I thought the teacher knew me, after all.

Within a month after I entered the school, I made a new discovery as to a schoolboy's equipments. I had thought that they consisted only of books, copy-books, an abacus, and such things. But these form only a half of them. The other half are hidden to view: they are in the pockets, or in the sleeves, I should have said. During the recess a strong cord will come out and also a top about two and a half inches in diameter, and with an iron ring a quarter of an inch thick. A Japanese top is a mad thing. When it sings out of the hands and hits that of the opponent, sending it off crippled, it makes you feel very happy. Another thing is a sling. It is as old as the time of David, but it was perfectly new to me. When a pebble shoots out and vanishes in the air, you feel as though you were able to hit a kite circling away up in the sky. And another thing! It is a knife, the broad-bladed one. With it they cut a piece one and a half feet long out of a thick branch of a tree and sharpen one end of it. Selecting a piece of soft ground, the boys in turn drive in their own pieces and try to knock over the others. The game depends much on one's strength and the kind of wood one selects. But there is a pleasure in possessing a cruel branch that will knock off three or four pieces at a blow. Oh, for a knife and a top! I thought. I disclosed the matter to my mother, who thought a top was all right and bought me one. But as for the knife, she gave me a small one, fit only to sharpen a pencil with. I felt ashamed (I blush to confess, though) even to show it to my schoolmates. If I had had money, I would have given my all just for a knife. But money was a mean thing; the possession of it was the root of all evil — so it was thought, and, indeed, I was penniless. But I must have a decent knife — decent among boys. If I could only get one I would give my Confucius for it.

One day I saw my Kichi — we had kept up our meeting ever since. I talked to him about a knife. He did not tell me how I could get one because I talked only about what the possession of a good knife would mean to a boy. It was a rather general remark, but I disliked to go right to the point. It would be too much to presume on his kindness, you know. And then I rather wanted him to offer. He, however, produced his own favorite knife and cut a thick piece of deal right away to show how sharp it was. Well, I thought he had a knife sense, anyway. So I kept talking about it day after day, and each time I talked of it he showed me his, and tried it on a piece of wood.

One day there was a town festival and in the evening I was allowed to go with Kichi to see it. Kichi's manner that night was very strange; he appeared as if he had a chestful of gold. He asked me in a fatherly manner what I liked, and said he could buy me all the booths if I wished him to. I never felt so happy as then. I thought my patience had conquered him at last. And to make a long story short, I came to own a splendid knife, better than any other boy's at the school! That night I slept with it under the pillow.

The next morning the first thing I did was to go to thank Kichi.

"Hello, Kichi," I shouted. "Thank you very much for the knife."

"Oh, good morning, Bot'chan. Let me see your knife," he said. "But I am sorry that I played a joke on you last night. It was your mother who paid for it. You must go and thank her for it."

"Well, never!" I gasped. But being told how she handed him the money when we started, I gave him a slap — a mild one, though — on his face and ran immediately to my mother, thinking that after all she had something more than a mere knife sense.

CHAPTER IV

IN TOKYO

Where We Settled — A Police Stand — Stores —
"Broadway" — Illumination — The Foreign Settlement.

ABOUT two years after I entered the village school I had to leave it for good and all. My father, as I have said, was in mid-air between the heaven of old Japan and the prosaic earth of the new institution. He would fain have remained there, had he had a pillar of gold to support him. And it is wonderful to see how this glittering pillar does support one in almost any place. It was a very serious matter for him to launch in the new current without any helpful equipment. But he had to do it, and made up his mind to try his fortune at the very centre of the new civilization, Tokyo. And so one day we said good-by to our friends who came to see us off, and started for the capital. "Parting is such sweet sorrow," as the poet sang, but I hardly remember now whether I shed tears or not. As I, however, look back to the day, I cannot but be grateful for the new move, for the immeasurable benefit it brought at least to us children.

In Tokyo we settled very near where my aunt lived. The street was by no means in a noisy quarter, but I can hardly think of anywhere in the city which was so well situated for being in contact with so many places of interest, at least for a boy just from the country. It was near to the "Broadway" of Tokyo, and just as near to the foreign settlement and to the railroad station, the only one of the kind in the city in those days. And if I wanted a touch of the old order of things, there was a big temple, a block on the east, which made its presence known to the forgetful people by striking a big bell every evening. I cannot say they rang the bell, because the bells at Buddhist temples do not chime, but boom. They are so big — bigger than a siege-gun. I liked the sound very much, as it brought to me like a dream the vision of a hillside sleeping under the setting sun. But I must not forget to mention a large piece of grassy ground very near us, where we could romp, fly kites, or play at a tug-of-war.

Now the first thing I did when I came to the new place was to familiarize myself with the neighborhood for the sake of running errands, or just to keep myself informed. First I started eastward and turned the corner to the left, where I found a wee bit of a house, or rather a box, six feet by nine, where two policemen were stationed. It was the first time I had ever seen any of them, and I thought they were a queer sort of people, who looked at me suspiciously whenever I looked at them in that way. But I thought as long as I did not do anything wrong, they would have no reason for coming at me. I also had great faith that if a thief should break into our house, they would soon come to our help. So I made several trials to see how quickly I could cover the distance to give them notice. They must have thought me a strange boy as I came panting to the police stand and stopped short to look at the clock inside.

A little beyond began the market. First a grocery store, then a fish stall, a bean-cake shop, and so on. I remember that the house I most frequented was a sweet potato store. I could get five or six nice hot baked pieces for a penny. And how I liked them! At regular intervals fresh ones were ready and we waited for them, falling into a line. When we got as much as we wanted, we would run a race lest they should get too cold. At the end of the street, just opposite a tall fire-ladder, standing erect and with a bell on the top, was a big meat store. Beef, pork, everything, they had, and sometimes I found a bill posted saying, "Mountain Whale, To-day." Whatever that might be, I never cared to eat such doubtful things. You never tried sea-horse or sea-elephant, did you?

Then, going in another direction from my house, I made my way to " Broadway." I first crossed a bridge which spanned a canal and came to an object of much interest. It was a telegraph-pole. I was never able to count the wires on it unless I did it by the help of a multiplication table, as there were so many of them, coming from all parts of the country to the central station. A strange thing about them was that they sang. When I put my ear to the pole, even on a windless day, I could hear a number of soft voices wailing, as it were. I thought they must come from messages running on the wires, many of which were indeed too sad to describe. And then there was something which made me think that boys in that vicinity had a very hard time. Many a time I saw kites with warriors' faces painted on them, entangled in the wires. The faces which looked heroic, now seemed only grinning furiously for agony! But I

THE JAPANESE "BROADWAY"

IN TOKYO. 41

must not be musing on such things, for if I did not take care in that crowded thoroughfare, a jinrikisha man would come dashing from behind with "Heigh, there!" which took the breath out of a country boy.

Broadway was built after a foreign style, — I don't know which country's, though. There were sidewalks with willow trees, — and there are no sidewalks in ordinary Japanese roads, — and brick houses, two stories high, and with no basement. Horse-cars were running, but they would not be on the track after ten in the evening. Many jinrikishas were running, too, and some half a dozen of them were waiting for customers at each corner. But not a shadow of a cab was to be seen anywhere. To tell the truth, I never thought of finding one then, its existence in the world being unknown to me at that time. There were a good many wonders in store for me in the shops, and I never grew tired of inspecting them. One curious thing was that here and there at the notion stores boys were playing hand-organs, probably to draw customers in. So I thought, anyway, and every time I passed I obliged them awhile by listening to their music. As I strolled on, I came across a sign with "Shiruko" in large letters on it. Shiruko is a sort of pudding, made of sweet bean sauce and rice dumpling, and served hot. To be sure, it made my mouth water, but I went on reading a bill over the wall. There were twelve varieties of shiruko, it said, styled after the names of the months, and any one who could finish eating all of them at one time, would get a prize besides the return of the price! How I wished that I had a big stomach!

The sight of Broadway was prettier in the evening, when the sidewalks would be lined with hundreds of stalls. I shall have occasion to describe them later, and so let me now mention one thing which I never remember without a smile. It was an illumination on a holiday evening — not of the whole street, but of only one building, and that of two stories, I remember. It was a newspaper office. And as newspapers are always giving us something new, this building, I think, awoke one morning to give us what was very new at that time. It girdled itself just once with an iron pipe half an inch in diameter, which twisted itself into some characters in the front, and awaited a holiday evening. The paper advertised that everybody should come to see how they were going to celebrate the holiday evening. So the whole city turned out, and all my folks, too. Hand-organs in the stores around began a concert, and people waited with their mouths open. The time came, and lights were seen running from both ends like serpents, closing up in the centre. Wonder of Wonders! "DAILY NEWS OFFICE" in gaslight appeared!

I must tell you one more adventure I had, and that was an excursion into the foreign settlement. As I came to the city I met with a foreigner once in a while. I wondered how I should feel if I but plunged into their crowd and spoke with them, if possible. So one day, with a curious mind, I started for the place where the foreigners lived together, about a mile from my home. As I neared the settlement I made several discoveries. First, the houses looked very prim and square, straight up and down, painted white, or in some light color. When viewed from a distance they looked as if they were so many gravestones in a temple yard. Unfortunately, it was the only comparison that occurred to a country boy. As I looked again, I found out another fact. That was, that while Japanese houses were nestling under the trees, foreign houses were above them. In fact, there was nothing more than low bushes around the houses. So my conclusion was that foreigners lived in gravestone-like houses, and did not like tall trees, being tall themselves, perhaps. As I entered a street I found everything just contrary to my expectation. Streets were deserted instead of being thronged; only one or two people and a dog were seen crossing. I went on, when, as luck would have it, I neared a Catholic temple from which two men, or women, — I could not distinguish which, — dressed in black, with hoods of the same color, came! How dismal, I thought, and immediately took to my heels till I came to another part of the street where the houses faced the sea. I wanted to see a boy or a girl, anyway, if I could not find a crowd. As I looked I saw something white at one of the gates, and what was my delight when I found it to be a little girl! I approached her, but not very near, as we could not talk to each other. I just kept at an admiring distance. I stood there, one eye on her and the other on the sea, lest I should drive her in by looking at her with both my eyes, and began to examine her. What a pretty creature she was! With her face white as a lily and her cheeks pink as a cherry flower, she stood there watching me. Her light hair was parted, a blue ribbon being tied on one side like a butterfly. She had on a white muslin dress with a belt to match the ribbon, but what was my astonishment to find that I could not see any dress beyond her knees! I could not believe it at first, but the dress stopped short there, and the slender legs, covered with something black, — I did not care what, were shooting out. Might not some malicious person have cut it so? "Oh, please, for mercy's sake, cover them," was my thought. "I don't care if you have a long dress, the skirt trailing on the ground." But was I mistaken in my standard of criticism? I looked at myself, and, sure enough, my kimono reached down to my feet!

CHAPTER V

MY NEW SCHOOL

Tomo-chan — The Men with Wens — A Curious
Punishment — How I Experienced It — Kotoro-kotoro.

OF course I attended another school as soon as we were settled. And every morning I went with my Tomo-chan.

But I must tell you who Tomo-chan was. She — yes, *she* — was the adopted daughter of my aunt, of about the same age as I, and in the same class at school. I wish I had space enough to tell you how she came to be adopted, but I shall have to be contented just with telling you that the main cause of her becoming a member of my aunt's family was all through me. Aunty had no child, but she had found how lovely a child is, even if he be mischievous, through my short visit two years before, which I have had no occasion to tell you about. Now one of the first principles in physics says that nature abhors a vacuum. This means that it is unnatural for a place to have nothing in it. I had gone back: who was to fill my place? So Tomo-chan, a better and certainly prettier child than I, slipped into my shoes.

Aunty wished us to be good friends. So I called on her every morning on my way to school, and in the afternoon we went over our lesson together. Arithmetic was not very hard for me, and so I helped her over pitfalls of calculation, while she did the same for me with reading. Girls remember very well, but do not care to reason things out, it seems. And indeed, Tomo-chan remembered even the number of mistakes I made in reading. Now what one can do in half a day, two can accomplish in half an hour, was the philosophy that came to me from our case; for our drudgery was over in no time, and we were going through Tomo-chan's treasure of nice pictures and books of fairy-tales. There was a picture in one of the books of an old man with a wen on his cheek, dancing before a crowd of demons and goblins. "Look here, what is this?" I asked. She laughed at the picture and would not tell me about it till she had thoroughly enjoyed laughing. That is the way of a girl. But with "O dear!" she started thus:

"One day, this old man with a wen happened to fall into a crowd of those ugly monsters, and was made to dance. He danced very well, and so was asked to come again the next day. The goblins wanted something for a pledge for his keeping his word and so removed the wen from the man's cheek. The old man was very glad to part with it, and went home, when he met another man with a wen." She turned the leaf to show another picture. This time the new man was dancing before the weird crowd. "You see, this man was told how he could remove his wen, and is now showing his skill before them to induce them to ask for the pledge. But he did not have any practice at all in dancing and so was just jumping round. And the goblins got angry over his deceit, and sent him back with the wen that the old man had left." Turning the leaf, "Here he is with wens on both his cheeks!"

MY NEW SCHOOL. 47

She laughed again, and I could not help laughing with her, too. At this moment some one was coming up the stairs.

"Why, is this the way you study your lesson?"

It was aunty who entered the room as she said: "I am surprised at you." And she laid down a tray with a teapot and cups and a dish of cakes on it. The sight made us happy all at once, and Tomo-chan explained to her how soon we had finished our study.

"Why, Ei-chan helped me in arithmetic, so we finished a long, long time ago."

"Well, Ei-chan is a good boy, isn't he?" said aunty. Boys feel awkward to be well spoken of to their face, and my speech failed me somehow. By the way, I was no longer "Bot'chan."

The school I found much larger and finer than the village one. The pupils numbered ten times more. Each class had its own room, and boys and girls marched in and out in procession every hour. It was so much more orderly and systematic than the village school that there was less of "out-of-tune" matter. But then there was one thing that puzzled me. It was that often a boy was seen standing in the hallway with a bowl of water in his hands. Sometimes he stood there motionless until the class was all dismissed. But I was not slow to divine the cause. What puzzled me was the question: "How could that be the best form of punishment?" While a boy stood there he need not attend the class. That was certainly easy for an idle boy. And then there was no pain to endure. As to the holding of a bowl, why, did I not hold my bowl of rice every meal and not know even if it was heavy or light? But another solution suggested itself to me; it might have the same effect on the offender as wearing a cap with "I am a Fool," written on it. He stood there, and everybody thought he was a bad boy. "It might be, it might be," I said, congratulating myself on the happy solution, when a crow that had just alighted on a branch of the elm by the gate repeated, "It might be!" I threw a stone at him without thinking that it was a violation of the school rule, and, if discovered, I might have undergone the punishment.

At any rate, I was destined, it appeared, to undergo the punishment once at least. And it happened in this way.

At this school, boys were not allowed to carry iron tops or even hand-balls. There were too many of them, and if they should all indulge in these sports, there would be constant danger of breaking their legs or knocking their noses off. So comparatively harmless footballs were provided. Now, one noon recess, ten of us wanted to have a game. We were divided into parties of five and played. Of course we had no rules to go by, but tried to carry the ball within the enemy's lines by every means. One time we fumbled furiously near the building, and, in the heat of our tackling, one fellow seized the ball and kicked it without minding in which direction he was aiming. If he had had less skill the ball would have gone only over the roof and dropped on the head of a jinrikisha man running on the other street. But as it was, it went madly against a window-pane and smashed it all to pieces. What a noise it made For a minute it made all the boys and girls playing on the ground keep quite still. And in this

MY NEW SCHOOL. 49

awful suspense a teacher appeared and caught the five, I among the number, who were still in the position of fumbling, together with the poor fellow who did the kicking, and who stood dazed, unable to recover as yet from the shock of his late experience. I didn't know how the other four escaped being caught, but I was glad that they did.

There was no question in the teacher's mind but that all six should be exhibited in the hallway, and so we were made to stand there, each holding a bowl of water. Now I had an ample opportunity to learn every significance of this form of punishment. Naturally, we felt merry at first. In the first place, there was something unreasonable and ludicrous in the way at least five of us came to stand there. And then when you have companions in your bad luck, you feel surely light of heart. And so we did. But when fifteen, thirty minutes passed, our legs got to be stiff and the weightless bowls began to weigh very much in our hands. Indeed, the slightest inclination would spill the water! But why did we not drink some of it, you may say? Well, we should have done it, but we knew that it must all be there when the teacher came. Forty-five minutes, and the bell rang for the dismissal. All the boys and girls poured out, leaving us alone. Ah, that is the saddest moment for any schoolboy, for after that the school is dismal as a prison. Fifteen minutes more, and all the teachers, except the one in charge of us, were gone. None of us dared to look up, our heads being bent with extreme sorrow. Presently a weak-minded fellow dropped his china and cried out. It was not I, but we were all ready to follow his example, when the teacher came out, and, removing the bowls, read us a lecture before sending us home.

We lost our courage, even to run out of the school compound, but dragged slowly home. But when I turned the first corner whom should I meet but my Tomo-chan?

"Why, Tomo-chan!" I looked at her in surprise.

"I could not go home without you. So I waited for you. But isn't it a shame for teacher to punish you without your deserving it?" she said.

"We did not want to let Takeda suffer alone, you know."

My answer was a surprise even to me. Of course, I did not think to the contrary, but I was not impressed with the significance of it till I put it into words and — to her. It came as a new thought to me. Our hearts became light, the thing was forgotten, and only the prospect of the fine time we should have that golden afternoon in late summer occupied our minds.

"Come along," I said. "Let's go to the field!"

And we hastened on briskly, and, throwing our things into our houses on the way, went to the field, green with cool, cushion-like grass. About a dozen boys and girls were already waiting for us, and we just jumped among them.

"What shall we play?"' said one.

"Let's have Kotoro-kotoro," suggested another.

"That's fun!" all shouted.

To play the game, we must first select from the boys one "chief" to protect his "sons and daughters," and one "imp" to catch them. The boys stand in a circle and are ready to say "Jan-ken-pon," and to ham-

MY NEW SCHOOL. 51

mer with their fists. At "pon" you make one of three shapes with your hand. When your hand is spread, that denotes a sheet of paper; when two fingers only are stretched, that means a pair of scissors; and when your hand is held closed, it signifies a stone. A sheet of paper can be cut by scissors, but the latter is ineffectual on a stone. But a stone can be wrapped by a sheet of paper. Hence, each one can defeat one of the rest, but is conquered by the other. To simplify the matter, you can use only two of the three shapes. The one who wins at first is to be the chief, the one who is ultimately defeated, the imp. So we began: "Jan-ken-pon!"

Only three won. Then those three tried again.

"Jan-ken-pon!"

I won; and so was the chief. The rest went on jan-ken-ponning till the imp was decided.

Now all except the imp held firmly each other's belt on the back, in a line, with me at the head. It is a pity you don't have any belt on your dress, and so play the sport. It is very convenient to us. Apart from its use in sport, when we meet a robber, we throw him down by jiu-jitsu, and, untying our belt, bind him up hand and foot! But to return. I was ready with the imp in front and with my "little ones" behind, like the body of a centipede. The imp could not touch me; he could only seize any one behind. I stretched my arms, ran to and fro to prevent the imp from getting round to my flanks. The line swayed, rolled, jerked like a serpent in a rapid flight. And the motion would all but throw weak-armed ones off their holds. But they merrily persisted, and could have held on longer but for their mirth being worked up too high by the very manner of the imp himself.

The boy who played that part was a born comedian. He loved his fun more than his bread. Once in the midst of his supper he heard a man come with a monkey dressed in a kimono. No sooner than he recognized that by the sound of a drum, he threw away his chop-sticks, and, running out of his house, danced all way up the street with the professional monkey as his wondering spectator. Now in playing his part as the imp, he did not go about it like an eagle intent on his prey. But he brought all his talent into full play in every motion of his body, suggestive of some grotesque form, heightened by a queer ejaculation. When, in his series of performances, he imitated a pig, flapping his hands from his head like large ears of the animal and grunting, Gr-r-r-r, Gr-r-r-r, it caused everybody to burst into laughter. At this moment he made a sudden turn, which caused such a jerk to the line, that, being absent-minded from merriment, they were all thrown out of their hold, each rolling on the grass, but still laughing at the grunting. The imp could now jump at anybody for his prey, but as a true comedian, he also rolled on the grass, laughing with the rest.

CHAPTER VI

CHINESE EDUCATION

My Chinese Teacher — How I Was Taught — Versification — My Uncle — Clam Fishing — A Flatfish.

SOME months after I entered the public school, my father came to a conclusion that what was taught there was too modern to have enough of culture value. My education had to be supplemented by the study of Chinese classics. And his intention would have been of great benefit to me if he had been equally wise in selecting a good private teacher. As it was, I gained but a fraction of it, undergoing a hard struggle.

There lived a Chinese scholar near by, who was second to none in his learning within three miles. Formerly he was a priest of Zen sect, the Unitarian of Buddhism. As it was considered most laudable to a man of his calling, he never ate fish or meat, and had two frugal meals a day, taking only a cupful of starch and sugar in the evening, till he came to lead a secular life. Starch and sugar ! — so he must have come to have such white hair, I thought. Anyway, the snowy mass heightened the expression of his earnest face, rather youthful for a man of sixty. He was, indeed, the classic itself; the rhythm of it seemed to be ringing in his veins, whether awake or asleep. And he delighted in nothing so much as to eat his dinner listening to the

CHAPTER VI.

clear-voiced chanting of boys reviewing their lesson, as if they were minstrels entertaining at a king's feast! And, of course, I was sent to him.

I started from the beginning, which was, indeed, no beginning at all. The Chinese sages did not write their scriptures as graded school text-books, but their descendants believed so, anyhow. Genesis was the genesis of successful mastery. And so I began with that great sentence in the "Book of Great Learning: "

> "Learning is a gateway to virtue."

I envy those boys who tore Chinese authors, and whose books, when taken to a second-hand bookstore, were not bought even for a penny. My books were, on the contrary, just as clean as ever, as if they had been too loath to impart anything to the owner. And this was not from any effort on my part to take care of them, but simply from the little use I made of them. Now this was the way I studied them. Teacher would read with me about four pages in advance, and see once how I could read. I stuck; he prompted me; I stuck again; he prompted me again; I stuck for the third time, and for the third time he prompted me, and so on, and indeed continually, if I had gone on till I had thoroughly mastered it. But one review seemed to him sufficient for such *easy* passages, and my boyish heart responded too gladly to be released after a short lesson. And I laid my book by till the next day. I did not know how the teacher regarded me, but he must have thought me a very bright fellow for whom such a slow process as review was totally unnecessary. And

CHINESE EDUCATION. 55

he immediately took up the next four pages and went on in the usual manner. The first book was finished; the teacher's instinct asserted itself, and he wanted me to read a few pages by way of a test before I proceeded. What a shame! I only recognized a box here and a starfish there, and that was all. The teacher was angry at the result. He saw that I was not prepared yet to take up the classics. And with his admirable pedagogical insight, he sent me to a primer the very next day. It was a Japanese history, written in easy Chinese prose. How I enjoyed the change! The passages rolled off on my tongue as easily as you might say, "Mary had a little lamb." The teacher smiled at my ease, and soon recovered his humor. But his eyes were so constructed as to see nothing but the top and the foot of a mountain, and his mind worked like a spring-board, which either stays low or jumps high up. And on the third day I was ordered to begin the second book of the classics, called the "Doctrine of Mean!"

And I plodded on. I went through the "Book of Divination," and "Odes of Spring and Autumn," and came out only with some phantoms of angular, mysterious hieroglyphics dancing before my eyes. But my Chinese education included something more than reading. It was versification. Just think of requiring a ten-year-old boy to write verse in Latin or Greek. But every Saturday I was required to do the same sort of thing for two years. Oh, how I struggled! I hunted for something sensible to write, but while all sorts of nonsense would come up, even common sense, that most useful guide in a prosaic field, fled from me. Outside, merry shouts of boys — a happy group who cared for balls

CHAPTER VI.

and kites more than dry-as-dust "culture" — were heard, and I mused in a corner of a room, consulting such help as a phrase book and a rhyming dictionary. Nothing but doggerel could be born of such a forced labor. Here is a specimen:

> "Shut from the blue of skies in spring,
>   I sit and fret for words to rhyme.
> O bird, if you have songs to sing,
>   Drop one for me to save my time!"

The Chinese training did me at least one good turn. It drove Confucius out of my head!

I should have been a blighted boy if Sundays had not come to my rescue. The real use to which the day should be put had not dawned on me, nor was it in the mind of those who introduced the institution. But I am glad to say that it did me good in many ways. With this, however, my uncle is invariably associated.

I have not said anything about him, but he was a well-fed man with a goat's beard. He was very nervous, however, and could not keep from pulling his beard. This accounted for its scantiness. It was very amusing to observe how easily his temper was disturbed out of its normal mood. When he was contradicted he pulled hard at his beard and wrung his hands furiously. His body seemed to expand with the inner fire when he ejaculated many an "Ahem!" preliminary to an eruption. Everybody had to find shelter and thrust his fingers into his ears, lest the drums should break. But when he was pleased, his face melted with laughter; he went to a cupboard to look

CHINESE EDUCATION. 57

for some nice thing for us, ordered dinner to be hurried for our sake, and went round and round us to see if we were really comfortable.

He was very alert, and was always looking for a new thing. He did well, too, to keep himself abreast of the age, and, indeed, mastered something of the English language, of which he could well boast in his day. His pronunciation, however, was rather painful to hear, and in his talk with foreigners his nervous hands played a large part to fill in the gaps in his vocabulary, with an intermixture of many a "you know."

One good thing about him was his love for outdoor sports. He could not sit all day like my Chinese teacher, and if ever an eruption occurred, it was always on the occasion of such confinement to his room. His Sundays were scheduled for this or that kind of pleasure excursion. And of course I was wise enough to do what I could to please him in order that I might not be left out of his party.

One Sunday we were to go clam-fishing. When it was announced on Friday before, I thought of a great time and could hardly sleep for joy. After a tedious labor of writing verse was over the next Saturday, I busied myself the rest of the afternoon with the preparation for the next day. I kept going to my uncle's to see whether we had the same things that they had, and also to suggest the necessity of providing things we had and they had not. Many conferences for this purpose were held at the door-sill with Tomo-chan. Small hand-rakes were bought, one for each; small and large baskets, knives, thick-soled socks, Small sashes, and so forth, were collected from various sources. To this

I added a net three by four feet large, with two poles to meet the exigency of encountering some large fish — perhaps a whale. But of this I did not speak to anybody.

Mother was also busy preparing our lunch. For this she got up very early in the morning and boiled rice, which she made into triangular, round, or square masses, speckled with burned sesame seeds. She packed them in several lacquered boxes, with fresh pickles and cooked vegetables. We relied on our clams for chief dishes; so some cooking utensils were necessary. Also some tea and a teapot, cups and dishes, together with chop-sticks and toothpicks, even.

The day was not fair, but it was just the kind of weather for the season, dull and somewhat hazy, but bespeaking a calm sea. The tide was fast ebbing when we started in a boat. There was a good company of us, including uncle, aunt, mother, Tomo-chan, and me. As we emerged into the bay from the canal, the extended view was delightful. On one side green masses of pine-trees overhung the stone mounds and merged into a leafy hill, which stretched itself like an arm into the sea. On the other, beyond reedy shoals, the old forts, with a lighthouse on one of them, dotted the expanse. The view was washed in gray, and even the sails of junks, hanging lazily from the masts, were scarcely lighter than the background.

All was calm. But as we sighted from a distance some other parties already on the scene, we soon forgot everything for the excitement and let the boatman hurry with all his strength. It was nine when we arrived at the desired spot, and we had three hours to enjoy ourselves. We fixed our boat to a pole, from the top of which was drooping a piece of red and white cloth. This served as our mark to enable us to find the boat quickly in the case of need. So each party had some thing of its own design. Purple, green, white, and red in all sorts of combinations and forms were displayed, while a coat, a shirt, or even an improvised scarecrow was not denied use.

So we went into water, our sleeves and skirts being tied up and our legs bared to the knees. Each was provided with a basket and a hand-rake — except myself, who, in addition to the implements, took out secretly my net, wound round the poles. My people were all too busy to observe me, however. We went on raking for clams. There seemed to be lots of black or white shells which we did not want, but I soon found that clams were rather a matter of chance, and a chance would come no more than once in every fifteen minutes I luckily struck on three nice ones in a short time, and dug diligently for some thirty minutes, but without any result. So I grew tired, and began inspection. Aunt had ten, mother eight, and uncle five. When I approached him, he looked up, red in the face. I wondered if he was not angry. But it was not so, for he heaved a sigh and straightening up and striking his back with his fist, said, "O dear! "

" Uncle, you will soon be quitting your job, just as I shall, I think," said I.

"Pshaw! How many have you?"

"Three, sir."

"You can't have more than that for your lunch, you understand, unless you get more. Now don't be in my way." And again he doubled his corpulent body to work. But I was right in thinking that he could not keep himself in the same posture for another three minutes. Now I passed on to Tomo-chan. Poor Tomo-chan had only two! She was all but weeping for the bad luck. She, however, looked comforted to find that I did not fare much better. But what was her surprise when I threw all my clams in with hers!

"Keep them, Tomo-chan. I am going to fish with this net." Her eyes looked gratitude. "Oh, thank you ever so much. But I'll catch fish with you if I don't fare any better."

"All right." And I went on thinking that if I could not get clams for my lunch, I should have fish to the envy of all. I looked among the rocks for some shadow of them. Surely I saw something shooting away now and then, without waiting for me to find out whether it was large or not. But anyway, they were all right if I could get a number of them, and so I fixed my net and tried to drive them into it, little thinking that the very whiteness of my net — I appropriated a net made for the purpose of keeping flies off — scared every fish. I got irritated with my ill-success, and finally splashed the water vigorously to punish them.

By this time my uncle had quit his work, as I predicted, and was engaging with hen-like anxiety to look after his flock. He kept his eyes on them, and would go like a shepherd dog to fetch any one who went too far away from the boat. He looked at his watch to see if the tide was not turning on, and went occasionally to the boat to see if anything was lost. He seemed to like this kind of work better than clam-fishing, for I

A Typical Japanese Street

could see even from a distance that he was pulling at his beard, as he was wont to do when his mind was occupied. Presently he heard me splashing the water far away, and started at once to bring me back. Time could not be lost, he must have thought, but I did not know anything of his approach till I heard a shriek behind me. Surprised, I turned round when I found him just recovering his balance and looking intently into the water.

"What's matter, uncle?" I hastened toward him.

"Stop. A flatfish somewhere." Seeing me with a net, he exclaimed, "Quick with your net."

"A flatfish?" I queried in excitement.

"Yes, I stepped on him and he gave me a slip. . . . Oh, here he is; cover him quick!" And we covered him with my net without much ado. I was surprised to see how easily I could catch him compared with other fish that I had tried for. As I raised him, however, I found he was already crushed dead under my uncle's weight!

But it was a large one, and I could have an honorable share at lunch.

CHAPTER VII

AN EVENING FÊTE

My Father – His Love for Potted Trees — A Local Fête —
Show Booths — Goldfish Booths — Singing Insects —
How a Potted Tree Was Bought.

EVENINGS were not without enjoyment for me. And for this I owe much to my father.

My father was a silent, close-mouthed man. His words to children were few and mostly in a form of command. They were never disobeyed, partly because it was father who spoke, but more because we knew that he spoke only when he had to. Indeed, he carried a formidable air about him, apparently engrossed in thought somewhat removed from his immediate concern. He was by no means philosophical, however, and his reticent habit was born of the peculiar circumstances under which he was laboring. Fortune was evidently against him. And partly out of sympathy with him and partly out of fear of breaking his spell, when we had something to ask of him — boys have many wants — we had some indirect means to devise. Thus, when my cap had worn out and I wanted a new one, I dropped a hint in his presence by way of a soliloquy: "I wish I had a new cap. My old one is worn out." Saying this just once at a time and thrice in the course of one evening, if I persevered for three nights, I used to have my old cap replaced with a new one on the next day !

He knew that he was fighting against odds, but his spirit was never crushed. He only persevered. One day he came back from his evening stroll with a piece of bamboo flute. Evidently he was attracted by a tune a man at the corner of a street was playing on it as he sold his wares, and felt his soul suddenly gain its freedom and soar to the sky. I remember how well he loved his instrument, and from day to day he used to pour out low, mournful tunes. But his art was never equal to the demand of his soul, and one evening the bamboo flute was laid aside for a pot containing a dwarf pine-tree.

You may well wonder how a flowerless potted tree could be preferred to even the commonest tune for spiritual solace. But at any rate it was a piece of nature, and was healing to behold. And then, in its fantastic shape, there was a beauty of repose which had a very soothing effect, but which required some study for appreciation. But in his case, there was something deeper in the matter. A tree over fifty years old, which, if left in the field, would have grown to an immense size, was reduced by human art to only a foot in height, and was kept alive on a potful of earth. My father must have read a history of his own in it and tried to learn a secret of contentment from it.

One by one potted trees were added to his stock, -he could afford to buy only at odd intervals, — and presently shelves were provided for them in the small garden. Morning and evening he attended to them, and with patience as well as with pleasure looked forward

AN EVENING FÊTE.

to the time when his care would result in a growth of just an inch and a quarter of pine leaves and palm leaves two inches by three in size.

One night an unexpected thing happened. A thief found his way to the garden from the back door and sneaked away with half a dozen of the choice trees. Naturally, my father was distressed, but after a while he was patiently filling the vacancy one by one, of course seeing that the back door should be securely locked every night.

I was going to tell you something about the amusements I had in the evening, but it was mainly due to this love of my father's for potted trees that I was taken regularly to a local fête, held three times a month. The day for this was fixed; it fell on every day connected with the number seven; that is, the seventh, the seventeenth, and the twenty-seventh. And as in the calendar, rain or shine, it came and went. Naturally, I had my weather bureau open on that day to see if the evening was all right, for a wet night would be an irretrievable loss. At the police stand they published a forecast in the morning, but that was not to be too much relied on. It sometimes said rain when it was anything but wet, and fine when it was actually drizzling — though in the latter case I rather inclined to believe the report even if it ended in sorrow.

I did not need any formality of asking to be taken; it was a matter of course with me as long as I behaved well. This behaving, however, was peculiar. I had to be waiting for my father outside and follow him when he came out, without saying anything or shouting for delight for a block or so. The reason for this was simple.

CHAPTER VII.

Mother objected to sending out the younger members of our family in the evening, and especially to such a crowded place where they were liable to be lost. My going there must not attract their attention.

One evening I slipped off with my father in this way. The place where the fête was held was not far away, and after two or three turnings we soon came to the street. At a distance, you might take it for a fire, for the tiny stalls and booths crowding the place were lighted by hundreds of kerosene torches which flared and smoked. The central section of the street was not more than two blocks in length, but it was literally packed with six rows of booths and stalls and with such a concourse of people that there did not seem to be room even to move.

The approach to the scene was marked by some show booths. Hung in front were some wonderful pictures of what was to be seen within: a serpent over thirty feet long, which had lived in some distant part of the country and had actually swallowed two babies; a woman who had a real rubber neck which could be stretched so far that while sitting still her head could wander all over the house; monkeys dressed in old-style costume and giving some theatrical performance, and so on. The entrance fee was a penny, and men stood outside crying the various excellencies of their shows, and when you stopped before one of them and looked at the sign, they would lift the curtain for a second and drop it again, just to whet your curiosity. I naturally wanted very much to look at some of the monstrosities, and watched to see if the inducement would work on my father, but, much to my disappointment, he walked calmly on with his hands in his sleeves.

Now we came in front of the goldfish booths. It was simply fascinating to see such a number of dear little things swimming in wooden tubs, some being hung high in glass globes by the side of helpless turtles enjoying air riding. In the next two or three booths were masses of minute bamboo cages. Most of them were only three inches by two. Here they were selling all sorts of singing insects and fireworms. And what an orchestra these tiny winged things were! There were bell insects which chirped on "chinkororin, chinkororin," in staccato, crickets which hummed in sweet undulating "rin — rin — rin," and katydids which broke in with a cymbal-like "gaja, gaja," as we say. I watched to see if these things would tempt my father, but no, his face was set on something else ahead.

Now a great part of these enterprising peddlers were gardeners by profession. And out of the six rows of booths in the central portion three were shows of potted flowers and trees. They even had for sale grown-up trees half as tall as a telegraph pole! As we came to this part my father slackened his pace. Here was something at last which interested him. He took time to examine some of the nice potted trees, and his progress was very slow indeed, somewhat to my annoyance. I would rather have him stop before a candy booth than in these places. After a while, however, he found one tree much to his liking. He was tempted just to ask the price of it.

"Ten dollars, sir," was the answer.

My father smiled dryly and passed on.

"How much you give, Mister?" asked the man.

No answer.

"I'll make it five dollars this time, Mister," cried the man. Still receiving no answer, he came after us. "But give me your price, Mister."

"Fifty cents," said my father.

"Ough, that won't pay even the express. Give me a dollar, then."

But my father was already some distance away. The man, growing desperate to lose him, cried aloud:

"Mi-ster, you can have it for the price. This is the first one I have sold this evening. I must start the sale, anyway."

So my father came into possession of one more potted tree. The price was low, to be sure, but the man did not undersell his goods.

There seemed to be nothing now to do but to wend our way home as my father turned round at the corner and came down with the crowd. We passed toy booths, basket booths, booths where hairpins with beautiful artificial flowers were sold, or where all sorts of fans, bamboo screens, and sundry other things were for sale. And we passed them apparently without any interest, at least on my father's part. I was wondering what my father would buy for me, when whom should I meet but my aunt and Tomo-chan just going round the street in the other way? I spoke with Tomo-chan while my father and aunt were exchanging some remarks — possibly about the potted tree.

"Did you get something bought for you?" I asked.

"No, not yet. I've just come, you know. And you?"

"N-no. But — "

I could not say the rest as my father and aunt parted and the crowd was pushing between us, and so I waved my hand to say good-by to Tomo-chan.

We soon came almost to the end of the gay portion of the street, and after a few booths a touch of festival air would be gone, when my father halted before a molasses candy booth, and, to my great joy, bought a nickel's worth of cake. We got a big, swollen bagful; this was for me and for our stay-at-home folks. I wished that I had met Tomo-chan once more.

CHAPTER VIII

SUMMER DAYS

A Swimming School — How I Was Taught to Swim —
Diving — The Old Home Week — Return of the Departed
Souls — Visiting the Ancestral Graves — The Memorable
Night — A Village Dance.

THE third summer in Tokyo had come. The air was fresh and cool, while the morning-glories in our back yard were blooming lavishly, and the Ainu chrysanthemums in white, pink, and purple, and the late irises were seen carried round the street in flower-venders' baskets. But it soon got warmer as they vanished from the sight till I found it hot even in one piece of a thin garment over my body, though my mother starched it for me just stiff enough for the air to pass through from one sleeve to the other.

In one of the canals near by, an annual swimming-school was opened. The place was inviting in hot weather, besides, it was such fun to bathe with hosts of boys, and to learn how to swim. I must confess that I could not swim yet. I thought at first that it was quite an easy thing, because I often saw a man swimming with his feet and performing such a trick with his hands as peeling a pear with a knife and eating it. But after a few trials I was obliged to correct my notion to such a degree as to consider swimming an extremely difficult as well as dangerous undertaking. Not only my body was found to be something between a block of hard wood and a stone, and much nearer to the latter, but once it stayed so long in the water, head and all, that I experienced pretty nearly what it was to get drowned. But all this I did in secret and did not tell to any of my folks. Indeed my mother was keeping my younger brother from the water by telling him about the story of a sea-monkey who would stretch his exceptionally long arm and drag people into the depths, especially boys who went swimming against their mother's remonstrance. As an elder brother, I was bound to set a good example.

A week after the opening of the school, however, I brought the swimming matter to my mother's attention, and piling up such reasons as I thought most expedient, and rounding up by mentioning names of a number of my schoolmates, as if they were co-petitioners, who had been enrolled in the membership, I wanted her to ask my father. I had anticipated a refusal from both mother and father, but my mother was all right as long as the place was safe, while my father surprised me by his instant permission. He was an excellent swimmer himself and must have felt it a shame that his son did not know even how to keep himself afloat. My poor younger brother, however, was to wait another year.

So I went to swimming. We had an exciting time in the canal, and the heat of the sun ceased to be of any trouble to me. On the first day one of the trainers supported me with his hands and made me move my arms and legs according to his instruction. I made a vigorous effort, while he carried me on as if I were making a progress myself. Now and then, however, he would loosen his hold and see if I could keep myself going. I was then taken with sudden fear, and, feeling that the water grew instantly to be very deep, I gave a cry of horror and distress, and did some splashing, too. The instructor laughed over my plight and told me that I should be safe as he was near, and that I must try to acquire the sense of ease with the water. As long as my limbs were moving properly, I was sure to be floating. So I put confidence in his words and cultivated assiduously what he called the sense of ease, which I understood to be a suppression of fear. The first day, how ever, passed without any result, in spite of my determination that I would go to the bottom rather than call for help again.

But, strangely enough, at the very first unassisted trial on the second day, my body did float. How joyful I felt at this, you can hardly imagine. I swam round and round the place — of course stopping every quarter of a minute — till I was fairly exhausted. On my return home, however, I mustered courage enough to impart to my brother on the matted floor my successful experience in swimming.

Diving came next. On my first dip I felt instinctively that man and fish were at the opposite extremities of creation. The suppression of breath and the closing of eyes were bad enough; but there was such a roaring in my ears as if all the watery spirits were murmuring at the intrusion, while my body was at once subjected to a different law of repulsion. But it was great fun to play at being a sea-monkey and drag the legs of idle boys, at which sport I had been a victim myself on the very first day. So I began practising it, and in a few days was already looking for a chance to apply my half-mastered skill. Seeing once two boys near me engaging in splashing water, I plunged at once, aiming at one of them. It was but a few yards to dive, but I came out of the water with out striking anything, and before I had time to brush off the dripping water from my eyes, I was subjected to a furious spray from the two boys, when, thud, came something on my side, and in another second I was dragged into the water. A mouthful of water went down my throat before I knew, and when I came to my feet with all the water boiling around me, I noticed a third and new boy standing and laughing over his trick!

So passed a good part of the summer till about the middle of August, when the Japanese "Old Home Week" came. The principal day falls on the sixteenth day of the seventh month, according to the lunar calendar, which is about a month after the ordinary date. It is a sort of Decoration Day, too, because we go to the temple yards and pay a visit to our ancestral graves. Now for three years this duty was neglected by us, and father thought it proper for some one to visit the old place in the country. My uncle was also in a similar position, and it was arranged that my aunt and Tomo-chan should go from their family while I represented my own. And two days before the date we set out in a conveyance called a kuruma.

I wasn't quite sure of the significance of the graveyard visiting on this special occasion, and so found time to ask my aunt of it. And this was what she told me, not on the road, but in her house the night before we started. (I had known the inconvenience of the kuruma in keeping me separate from my aunt all the way, though it had the decided merit, as it turned out, of packing Tomo-chan and myself in one seat.)

Now, when a man dies, he goes either to paradise or to hell, according to Buddhism. In the former place, he is led to his seat on a large lotus flower floating on the cool surface of the rippling water. The sweet calmness of the summer morn is all his, my aunt said, but beyond that there seems to be nothing going on in that floral berth. But in hell, all is excitement. The king of devils will mete out punishment to each arrival according to his guilt, and he is made by red and green demons to tread on the hill of swords, to ride in the coach of fire, or to bathe in the boiling caldron. But, good or bad, those departed souls are allowed once a year to pay a short visit to their earthly homes, and this happens on the sixteenth of the seventh month. So we go to the graves of our ancestors, clean and decorate them so that the dead may feel comfortable, and, delivering our message of welcome and turning about, ask the invisible to get on our backs to our homes! I wondered if my back was large enough for the whole train of my ancestors to ride on.

At my native village we stayed at another uncle's. A day's ride in the same narrow kuruma made Tomo-chan and me more companionable than ever, while the strangeness of the new place kept us two always close by. Everywhere we were welcomed as Tokyonians, and treated to melons and rice dumpling. We had not, however, much time to spare, for we were quite busy seeing to our family graves. We hired a man to weed and clean the lot, sent enough offerings to the temple so that the priests, when chanting for the rest of the departed, might think comfortably of it, and, above all, took care that every grave might not lack fresh flowers for two days, that is during our stay. On the sixteenth day I was prepared to carry any number of invisible spirits from the graveyard to the house. But as some one told me that the spirits would not dare to come in the daylight, I was glad that my service was not needed, after all.

The sun set gloriously behind the castle, and the mellow booming of the temple bell was wafted through the evening air. Presently the misty moon, just waning, rose from the plain, and the memorable night began. In every house the rooms were swept clean and the tiny lights were burning in the household shrine. In front, the flames from a heap of flax stems, known as the "reception fire," were dazzling, and, unheard and unobserved, the ghosts of our fathers passed into the house.

I did not know how long they would stay, but bowing once respectfully before the shrine, I went out with Tomo-chan to stay around. In the temple ground there was an open space hemmed in by tall, shady pines, where the young people of the village would assemble that night and hold the annual dancing. And naturally our steps were directed there. We found that already many of them were gathered, and, by the uncertain light of paper lanterns hung here and there on the trees, we saw that they were all dressed in uniform white and blue garments, with folded pieces of cloth dangling about their necks. The browned faces of the swains were not distinguishable in such dimness, but those of the lasses looked distinctly lovely, the scratches and blemishes incidental to their outdoor occupation being invisible. The swains grouped on this side and the girls on the other; the former being not yet bold enough, and the latter too shy, to mingle with one another. Presently some sweet-voiced lad sang a ballad, and then all rose to arrange themselves in rows, boys on one side and girls on the other. They called to the singer to start anew, and began to trip to the song, clapping their hands at a rhythmic turn. They never moved on, but closed in and again drew apart on the same spot, all repeating the same movement. It was a novel thing for both of us, and we watched them with great delight. Song after song was sung, all bursting into laughing cheers after each piece and sometimes going into such commotion that each lad paired with his bonny lassie.

"Isn't that delightful?" I asked Tomo-chan.

"Yes, lovely."

"And simple, too."

She nodded.

"Let's watch again and see if we can learn," I said to her, and we stood at the end of the line.

The song went clear and plaintive and the touching trill was preying upon the hearts of the dancers and working them into dreamy ecstasy. The moon by this time climbed high up in the sky, and when a filmy cloud glided off her face, the pale weird rays revealed Tomo-chan and me dancing in the group!

CHAPTER IX

THE ENGLISH SCHOOL

A Night at the Dormitory — Beginning English — Grammar — Pronunciation — School Moved — Mother's Love.

It was September and the beginning of a new term. Father decided that I should leave the school I had attended hitherto and go to another one where English was taught. This was the second time that I had left school without finishing it, but I was destined not to fare any better at the new place. Indeed, I changed school four times without finishing, till I finally settled in a college. But this leaping habit — I am sorry to say that it took a semblance of habit at last — did not come from any changeableness on my or my father's part, but all from the sincere desire to prepare me for life in the best way. This it was that drove me into the three years' study of the Chinese classics, though I beat a rather dishonorable retreat from it, and again this it was that directed me to take up the foreign languages early. I was afraid, however, that I leaped too much this time, as I found that all my new schoolmates were much older than I, and, indeed, there were some who needed shaving every morning!

The school was at first very near to my house. The building was of brick; the first floor was used for the class-rooms and the second was made into a dormitory. This last was a novelty to me; I never knew before that boys stayed away from home in this fashion, and entertained a secret desire to share a bed once with somebody, just to see what it was like. This, however, was easily granted, as I soon grew to be a favorite with everybody be cause of my youthfulness, and one night I made a bundle of my night-shirt and went to the room of one of my classmates. I was at once devoured with curiosity in watching him make the bed. It was not such a simple process as I used to see at home — laying one or two quilts on the matted floor and another over them. But he had to build a bedstead first from a sliding door, and placed one end of it on his table and the other on his bookcases. Upon that he laid his thin quilt and blanket. I wondered why he had to do such a crazy thing.

"Don't you know the reason?" He seemed to be surprised at my ignorance. "It is on account of the fleas. You can't sleep on the floor. Look here." And he showed me a bottle in which an army of captured fleas were drowned. After all, a dormitory was not a covetable place, I thought. But there was some fascination in the sliding door bed, which creaked like a cuckoo with every move of my body.

But I must tell you about my first experience in English. English was very encouraging to start with. The alphabet consists of only twenty-six letters, and when I mastered that and was provided with a handful of vocabulary, I felt as if I were already half an American. I went around and talked to everybody, especially to those who did not know anything of English, like this:

THE ENGLISH SCHOOL. 79

"It is a dog. See the dog! It is a cow. See the cow!" I could even play a trick by way of variation like this:

"Is it a dog? Yes, it is a dog."

And my family, who were constantly spoken to in this unknown tongue, were surprised at my speedy progress.

And indeed I thought first that any number of words might be easily learned, because they were but combinations of letters in one way or other, which are limited to only twenty-six. But it did not take me long to change this view. As the length of the daily lesson increased I came to wonder more and more whether the English words were not charmed after all. They were as slippery as eels, and, indeed, written like eels too. I thought time and again that I had them secure in my mental box, but when I opened the lid the next day, they vanished like a spirit. Something must be done, I thought, to tie them down, and so I invented a certain scheme. It was that when I looked up a new word in my Anglo-Japanese dictionary, I put a black mark beside it to show that on that very moment it passed into my possession. The plan seemed to work very well, but before long I found I had to mark the same words three or four times, till my dictionary looked very much as if it were suffering from spotted fever!

Then came grammar. Grammar is the least familiar part of language study. We are never taught in that in learning vernacular Japanese. Somehow words come out of our mouths naturally and arrange themselves into smooth sentences. So when I had to commit to memory the definitions of the noun, verb, adjective, and so forth, and to classify English words into them,

A Japanese School of the Present Day

I came to doubt if I were not studying botany instead of language. Fortunately I did not make such a mistake as, "A verb is something to eat," or "Every sentence and the name of God must begin with a caterpillar." But it took me months to understand the difference between the transitive and intransitive verbs. I finally struck an original definition of them. It is this, that a verb is called transitive when it is ambitious and intransitive when it is not, because in the former case it takes an object and in the latter it does not. I wondered why some one among the learned teachers did not tell me that right away in the beginning. It would have saved me a lot of trouble. Again in parsing, any word parading with a capital was a relief to me: I had no hesitation in giving it as a proper noun, whether it appeared in the main body of a piece or — in the title!

Now there is one little part of speech which puzzled me a great deal. It is the article. In translation I had the great satisfaction of passing it over entirely, as we have no equivalent to it in Japanese, but in composition it was the first thing that puzzled and annoyed me. The Japanese formerly went out bareheaded, and their language is also free from this encumbrance of a head-gear — for the article is a head-gear to a noun — and I was liable to drop off the article entirely, or, if I tried, to use a wrong one every time. Surely this hat etiquette was difficult and capricious, too. I thought I could master its secret if I knew thoroughly when and what sort of a bonnet a girl should wear — of course including the case of wearing a derby on horseback! This occurred to me a long time afterward in America, however.

Let me mention another difficulty. This was the pronunciation. A number of new sounds were introduced, the most conspicuous of which are those in which th, l, f, and v are found. The th– sound was bad enough, but l was next to impossible. Finding this to be the case, an American teacher would draw a cross-section of a face on the blackboard, only with a scant outline of the mouth and nose (once he drew the head, too, but it caused an unusual amount of merriment among the boys, as it was as bald as his, and he never finished the picture again), and explain the position of the tongue in uttering the sound, which we industriously copied. And he also would have us say, "Rollo rode Lorillard," instead of "Present," or "Here," when the roll was called. But the semi-historical passage fell from the boys' lips rumbling like a thunder:

"Rorro rode Rorirrard!"

One year passed happily in the new school, when it moved to its new buildings on the other side of the city, about five miles away. It was at first a short walk from my house, but when it increased from two minutes to two hours, with no convenience of street-cars to help my feeble feet, I naturally hesitated to go. I had to walk if I continued to attend, as boarding out in the dormitory was too expensive for our means. The school, however, was too good to be given up at that time, and so I made up my mind not to discontinue it.

To cover ten miles a day, spending four to five hours, was not a light task for a boy of thirteen. It was all I could do on fine days. In stormy weather the feat would become a struggle, and I was more than glad to accept the kind offer of one of my schoolmates to break the trip at his home for the night.

I had to start early to be on time at the eight o'clock exercise. Five o'clock was the time for me to get up, but my mother rose at least at half-past four to make me a hot breakfast of boiled rice and bean soup.

My mother was the sort of woman who expresses herself in work rather than in words. And in this she was regularity itself. One thing which impressed me in this more than anything else was her management of my dresses. Japanese decency requires eight suits a year for any one just for ordinary use, and of course I needed, or rather my mother believed that I needed that: eight suits — four in summer, two in winter, and one each in spring and in autumn. The dresses were not always made from new pieces, and so gave much more trouble. She made over the old clothes, washed and turned or dyed, if necessary, before doing so. My notion of her regularity, however, must be augmented five times, as she was doing the same thing — though I did not notice it at the time — with the other members of the family.

And so this early rising on her part for my sake went like clockwork morning after morning. If this means steadiness of her devotion to her son and to all related dearly to her, she had it.

Again she was not wordy in any case. I never had a long lecture from her, though, I am sorry to say, I had some short ones. On the contrary, she had the secret of speaking in silence. There was some magic power in her touch. I love to look back to my childhood, when she used to dress me in the morning, at the end of which she would whisper in my ear just a word: "Be good all the day, dear child." It was simply pleasure.

So at this hour when the world was still asleep, as I sat without a word at a short morning repast before her, with the lamp shining and every manifestation of motherly love around me, I was under an unspeakable spell, and learned to love her most.

I had to start soon, however. I descended to the door and opened it. It was still dark and the sky was starry. There was something that held me back for a moment. But I took heart and went out. Mother wanted to go with me for some distance. Naturally, I declined the offer, wishing not to seem cowardly, but also because I did not want to give her such a trouble. So she just stood at the door with a lantern and saw me off till I turned the corner.

I thought she turned and stepped inside after that, as I heard the noise of the sliding door being shut, and, being satisfied, I hurried on my way. But one morning something happened that revealed the truth. There was a bridge at the second turning, two blocks away from my house, and from that a long street ran. I was away some distance on this road when one of the fastenings of my clog-straps broke off. It is sad when this occurs. We cannot walk at all. We should be provided with material for repair, but it seldom happens that we are. To return was to lose time, and I must be going. So I did what boys usually do under such a circumstances. I hunted a wedge-shaped pebble, and, holding the broken end of the fastening in the hole, where it had been kept tight, drove it with another piece of stone. I was able to walk a short distance, but again it broke off. I was irritated, but there was no use in fussing: so I again went patiently to repair. I was hammering the clog with a stone when I heard the noise of hurried steps approaching. I was too busy to look back, but a voice came which made me drop the stone.

" Sakae! "

I turned, and there my mother stood with a strip of cloth ready to help me! I was surprised, but was too glad for help to ask any question.

As I trod on, I reasoned to account for her appearance in this way: that after seeing me turn the corner, my mother was wont to put out the light, shut the door, and follow me to the bridge, and from there was watching to see that I was safe. She saw that day that I was in trouble, and divined the whole case by the knocks I gave at the clog. So she was there with her help. As I thought of that, a silent tear trickled down my cheek.

CHAPTER X

A BOY ASTRONOMER

What I Intended to Be — My Aunt's View — My Parents' Approval — My Uncle's Enthusiasm — The Total Eclipse of the Sun.

Like all ambitious boys, I now began to dream of my future.

In a daily paper to which we were subscribing, there was a story appearing in serial form, which I happened to read, and in which I became immediately interested. It was a scientific novel, with a revenge motive. The title, the author, the plot — all are now forgotten except the vague idea that the hero in the end, by his high inventive ability, built a wonderful machine, by means of which he poured poisonous gas into the castle where his enemy lived, and thereby took his vengeance upon him. I was simply fascinated, and wanted to be an engineer.

The first one to whom I confided my intention was Tomo-chan. Of course I did not and could not depict an engineer as the one in the story, wrapped in the glowing splendor of his intellectual triumph. I might have tried it if she had given me a chance to do so. But too soon her peculiar and perhaps truer view of the profession came on me like a blow.

"Why, isn't an engineer a sort of carpenter?" she asked. Reduced to such a lowest term, even my hero looked shabby, and from that very moment I dropped him entirely.

I was not, however, fortunate enough to find a substitute worthy of my admiration, and I had to go without any. But this time my mind seemed to be able to present to me a proper object of my ambition. All my thought gradually drifted toward the province of science (I little knew then that it was the same engineer story which influenced me). Of all branches of learning, science appeared to me to be the most substantial, most worthy of serious study, and most certain of arriving at the secret of the creation. The study, however, of a small portion of God's work, such as a leaf of a tree or a nameless insect, did not appeal to me. No, any section of the earth was not large enough to lay down my life for. I wanted to take in the earth, the sun, the moon, the planets, and the stars — in fact, all the universe at once! So I fixed upon astronomy as my special study. The immensity of the field and the purely theoretical nature of the subject, coupled with the transcendency of the pursuit over the triviality of worldly affairs, had all its charm over me. It was simply great.

I went again to Tomo-chan to tell her of my intention. The idea of an astronomer was apparently beyond her grasp. She could not think of any occupation such as carpenter, mason, and so forth, to associate with an astronomer, and it did not take her long to admit that it was grand.

This was my first triumph, and now I approached my aunt to see what she would think of it. She was one of those women whose mind never soared above the world even for the sake of observation. She could not conceive the idea that this earth — which, by the way, was flat, according to her view — revolves every day. I went into a whole length of explanation by the help of a lighted lamp and my fist, to show how the revolution would cause day and night, but to no purpose. So I changed my tactics and told her the story of a little girl, who, in her own way, understood this fact. She lived at the foot of a high mountain, on the summit of which there was a lake. The little girl could not understand how water could be found in such a high place till she was told one day about the diurnal revolution of the earth. "That must be true," she said, "and so the mountain dips into the sea in the night and carries the water from there!"

But it was not my purpose to convince her about such a matter, and so I proceeded to acquaint her with my intention. I soon found that it was not exactly in the line of her approval. She presented to me at once her worldly view of the profession, how out of ordinary my choice was. The astronomer was to her a man who sleeps when all should be up, and is awake when all should be in bed. He looks always at the sky, and does not know often that he is about to tumble into a ditch. He has to perch on a roof or a tree-top like a sparrow, to watch the stars while everybody is enjoying some nice thing in the house.

This, however, had no effect of a wet blanket upon me. I knew that she was teasing me for the mere fun of it. Her humorous eyes were ready to take in any change in my surprised countenance, which on my part I partly assumed to please her.

A BOY ASTRONOMER.

In the end, however, she frankly admitted that the constantly increasing number of new studies in these enlightened days bewildered her greatly, and she could not tell which profession was sure to lead one to success. Perhaps I was right, she said, in choosing a study which only a few might attempt.

Two days passed, in the course of which I became surer of my choice and was ready to face my parents. I had a secret suspicion that my father might have some plan already laid out for me. If he had had anything in mind outside of a scientific pursuit, I should have been nonplussed. But, luckily, I found I was ahead of him; indeed, he and my mother, too, seemed to trust everything to my natural inclination, and had only a vague but bright future for me without any particular road leading to it. So, when I laid before them, side by side, my desire or rather my determination to become an astronomer and a future college professor, with an income four times as great as my father's, — I reserved the poetic side of my choice for my own meditation, — I made such a deep impression on them that it surprised me altogether. My mother, bending over her sewing by lamplight, silently passed her hand over her eyes, while my father picked up a paper which had been read all through, with a slightly drawn "Um," in his throat, which in his case was to be interpreted as indicating some pleasant feeling. My mother was the spokesman in such a case when my father's silence was meant for consent. She told me that one must go heart and soul into any sort of study in order to excel in it. I simply nodded, and presently went to bed with a light heart, after bidding good night to the dear little stars who would be my constant companions hereafter.

I could not meet my uncle till Sunday, but Tomo-chan told me that he heard everything about me from my aunt, and was very enthusiastic over my intention. Indeed, he was always enthusiastic over new things, though his enthusiasm was usually rather short-lived. But I was glad that my news struck him in that light. That morning I found him reading a paper, but as I approached he looked up, and, removing his spectacles, and combing his beard with his fingers, surveyed me awhile as if to see if I was capable of my word. But really he was waiting for the return of his enthusiastic mood. I felt that Tomo-chan was smiling over my situation from the next room, though I could not remove my eyes from my uncle.

"Astronomer, eh?" he said at last.

"Yes, sir. Going to be one."

"That's grand. You will be the fourth or fifth in that line in our country. I should take one of those new studies if I were young enough. But astronomy is indeed fascinating. Do you know that the moon never shows her other side?"

Here he rose up and began to pace the room. His enthusiasm served to bring back a flood of the shallow but ready knowledge which he stored up in a corner of his head. And he did not let me speak a word till he had finished a lecture on the solar system.

"Look here," — he turned to me with the look of a man who made a sudden discovery, — "do you know of the solar eclipse we are going to have on the 20th?"

Of course I did. It was still two weeks thence, and the moon was as opposite as could be, but I had already darkened a piece of glass over a candle and begun to observe the sun at least once a day.

"This is the total eclipse and its rare opportunity. You may not see it again in Japan in your lifetime," he went on.

In my lifetime was too strong a phrase, but I was very sorry to miss the chance, as the zone of the total eclipse passed some fifty miles north of Tokyo, and I had — no money.

"Perhaps in your lifetime, too," I ventured to suggest.

"Yes, indeed. I did not think of myself," he laughingly said. "Well, then, let's go!"

"Go?"

"I will take you and Tomo with me."

In the adjoining room Tomo-chan was seen just raising both her outstretched hands, opening her mouth, and rolling her eyes — all bespeaking her joy and surprise. I wished very much to answer the signal but for the presence of my uncle, who kept staring at anybody or anything near him, and this time at me, while revolving some new plan in his mind.

For the intervening days I was busy making preparations for the expedition. I had to buy half a dozen pieces of glass, frame and darken them in a variety of shade; to adjust my watch to keep time; to study the constellation where the sun was, and note the stars of the first magnitude visible on the day; and to make four or five copies of a drawing with a graduated circle in the centre for the sun, and two other concentric circles for the orbits of Mercury and Venus. The difficult part of the business was how to record time for the beginning of the eclipse. We needed two, at least, for this. Tomo-chan was glad to offer her service, but she did not want to look at the watch but at the sun. Well, I had no objection to that, as long as she could tell the right moment. But as I was a little in doubt on that point, we spent several nights in drill by means of a shaded lamp which cast a bright disc on the wall. No sooner than I moved an opaque one and touched the other, she had to press my hand. But too often the movable disc was a quarter of an inch inside the other when the belated touch passed on to me. So I had to train her eyes first by giving a signal at the time of contact by means of a pinch. And if she did not perceive it still, she got pinched still harder. She was very unteachable in this respect, but still wanted to look at the sun rather than the watch!

So the day of the eclipse arrived. It was a hot, clear day in July, and most fitted for the observation. We took an early train, as we had a long way to go, and then we must settle somewhere to watch the beginning and the end and the most precious middle. In the central part of the zone of the total eclipse there was a government observatory temporarily erected, and we wanted to get as near to it as possible. But we did not take into account the rather slow service of the train, and the hour for the eclipse had come before we got into the zone, and were, of course, in the train. As nothing could be done under such circumstances, we gave up the initial observation, and all the three just looked at the sun through the soot-covered pieces of glass. We did not know that we were a gainer and not a loser by this till late, except Tomo-chan, who had already earned enough pinches merely to be ready for the occasion.

The train was a few miles within the zone when my uncle thought it wise to stop at a small village and make an observation there, as the sun was fast being overshadowed. We settled in a nice tea-house, whose front room in the second floor with an open veranda was just the sort of place for our purpose. And there, after a quick lunch, we awaited the hour. Tomo-chan and I had a board and a sheet of paper which I had specially prepared, to note the location of the visible stars and to draw the shape of the corona.

I never knew that the light of the sun was so strong, for till the luminous surface was reduced to a very thin crescent, no change was observed in the sky. But all at once, as the shadow of a man passing on the street became weirdly faint, the color of the sky turned into warm steel-black and the purple stars began to shine! And in no time the crescent was changed into a mere speck of silver light, and in a second, as it burned itself off, a beautifully soft fringe of twilight appeared. That was the corona!

I now assiduously set about to take down the exact shape of it. There were only thirty seconds of this precious moment. So I just put down important points on the paper, noting carefully the position and the distance, and tried to take a clear impression in my mind to be traced out later. Tomo-chan was working, too. But her process was just the opposite of mine. Evidently she wished to follow my picture, but as mine was no picture, she turned to the sun with a sigh, and, though she finished it in time, she had a picture of a heavenly corona twisted considerably by an earthly wind!

The wonderful moment had now passed, and the corona, with a tail trailing at the right-hand side of the sun, disappeared like a dream. It was too brief, but we were satisfied, and did not know what to think of our good fortune when, three minutes later, a dark cloud came and brushed the sun off. Then we imagined what the consequence might have been if the train had been fast and we had gone on further north. The next day's paper said that the government expedition was entirely spoiled on account of the untimely shower!

CHAPTER XI

IN THE SUBURBS

A Novel Experiment — Removal — Our New House —
Angling — Tomo-chan's Visit.

We were now to remove to the suburbs. Father got a better position with a firm quite far from our house, and it was thought expedient for us to do so for his convenience.

There was one thing which made me dislike this change. And it was about Tomo-chan. We should be separated, and might not see each other so often; all the more so as we had grown to be quite intimate and congenial by this time and had great fun in indulging in some novel experiment now and then. This last was by no means of a scientific nature. Still we went at it with something of scientific spirit to see whether a certain innovation was applicable or not.

Here is one such experiment we tried. Tomo-chan heard from one of her friends, whose sister recently came home from America, that in that enlightened country when a lady and a gentleman take a walk together, the latter offers his arm to the former, who, of course, never hesitates to take it. Tomo-chan thought it was a fine idea, and asked me if we might try it. Well, I had no objection if it were only dark enough to make the trial. So one evening, under the shade of cherry-trees, we hooked our arms. Our cumbersome sleeves were somewhat in the way, but still we got on famously. After that, whenever we were in the dark, a hint would come from Tomo-chan to walk in that fashion, and I was only glad to accept it. Curiously enough it was the girl who suggested it every time!

Of course we were not uniformly successful. I well remember the evening of that memorable day of the total eclipse. My uncle's enthusiasm greatly abated as the event of the day passed, and as we alighted from the train and stood before a fruit-vender's stall, he now appeared to be much interested in a large watermelon. Unable to resist the temptation, he bought one and had me carry it. So I held it under my arm and walked on. The street was not crowded and the night was dark, and I went on behind my uncle with Tomo-chan beside me, when a touch was felt at my unoccupied arm. It was the well-known hint, and in no time Tomo-chan and the watermelon were hanging from my arms. It was not an easy thing to walk in that way, especially behind the back of my uncle, who might turn round to see us at any moment. Then I found that even a watermelon had a bit of jealousy in it, for every minute it would get heavier and more unmanageable as my mind inclined more and more to my fair companion. The point was soon reached when it was no longer endurable for the watermelon, and at my unguarded moment it jumped out of my arm to commit suicide. The bounce at once made my uncle turn and wring his hands for anger at my carelessness. I was equal to the occasion, however. Quickly extricating myself from Tomo-chan, I pounced at the sulky thing before a word was spoken, and saved it from any harm. So we went on as before. Only both my arms were now taken by the watermelon, and poor Tomo-chan dragged on crestfallen.

But such fun we could no longer have now that we were to be separated for a time at least, and we parted with heavy heart.

The removal was a curious affair. On five or six carts, everything in the house from paper screens to a kitchen stove was piled up. There was an old pomegranate-tree in the back yard which we had brought from the country some six or seven years ago. And of course we dug it up carefully and loaded it on the cart. Also we did not forget to pull down long poles for drying purpose and add them to the heap, together with two or three round stones for pressing pickles. The train of the carts pulled by coolies then moved slowly on through the city, and it was after dark before we could unload them at the destination.

The new house was in a charming spot. Just back of us was a low hill thickly wooded with tall oaks and criptomerias; to the left across a brook stretched a tilled field, fringed in the far distance with bamboo bushes and elm groves; to the right and on the hill the eye could command the western horizon where Fujiyama hung low like an azure fan against the golden sky. The birds sang, the flowers bloomed, the fire-worms glowed, and I never felt a change so delightful, coming as I did from a town where boys believed that Indian corn either grew on a tree, or sprang, like bamboo shoots, from the ground without planting.

My school came to be much nearer; the potted trees of my father increased; a baby was added to our family; and, as the sun and the moon moved on peacefully, we were all well contented with our lot.

There was not much to be recorded for our purpose in those days except the angling my father and I had occasionally in a river. His was always a calm turn of mind, and the soothing, restful pastime of fishing suited him immensely. I love to picture him sitting under the sheltering pine-tree by a quiet river bank, and handling the rod and line, while quaint ripples of smiles came and went across his face as the nibbling fish gave his line a tantalizing pull. Once, when it was the season of smelt in the month of May, we went over to a stream about two miles off. The scene around there was lovely. The mass of fresh leaves covered the open field, and along the slope of the bank, with stunted willows here and there, myriads of dandelions like golden stars studded the green. And the breeze was fanning leisurely the warmth of the May sun. The stream was shallow, and was singing and foaming on the pebbly bed.

"Let's see what we can do about here," said my father, as he selected a spot where the water was going on in a cataract. And we cast our flies and tried our luck. But, after awhile, having no success, I began to doubt if my father had chosen the right spot, and so I thought that I had better follow up the river and see if they bit. I left my father to his fortune and started on my adventure. I did not know that smelt-fishing was such a dull business, for, wherever I went, there was the foaming pool, the steady flow, and there were practically no bites. Yes, there was one, but I only fished a piece of some rotten wood or dripping moss! I wondered what my father was doing, and, not without a smile over his probable ill-luck, I went back, when I found him still standing in the same spot. I doubted if he was not going to take root there. I at once inquired about his success. "No, nothing remarkable," he gently replied, dreaming on the sparkling water. I went to his basket dipped in the river, and lifted the lid, when a large prisoner, disturbed by the jar I gave, snapped violently! After all, I thought, he was of a piece with Izaak Walton.

So days passed, and more than a year rolled on since our removal. It was now the latter part of October, when one day we had unexpected visitors. They were my aunt and Tomo-chan. This was not their first visit since we came here, but I had always been out and had had no chance to meet them. Still, they did not come very often, and so my aunt, with many bows, apologized for her negligence to call, while my mother, with equal courtesy, was not behind the guest in heaping up apologies for neglect on her part. Then, as tea and cakes were produced, inquiry after the health and condition of each member of the family issued from both sides, and was answered modestly, followed by amiable comment from the inquirers. Then, with equal lightness of heart, the season was talked over, the recent events, and, indeed, anything of timely interest.

While such a talk was going on my eyes were secretly on Tomo-chan. I was surprised at her change. I left her a mere child only a year and a half ago, but the bud of yesterday was the flower of to-day. With a snowy neck and rosy cheeks, her ebony hair done up stylishly, she sat in striped silk of light azure and dove-gray. She no longer looked at me straight, but, except for furtive glances, her eyes sought her jewelled hands, idly occupied in clasping and unclasping on her knees. A glow of bashfulness was beaming from her as most eyes sought their focus in her.

As the talk was about to become more personal, my mother suggested that Tomo-chan might go out with me as a guide to look around the place, which was beautiful at that time. My aunt seconded the motion, and asked me to take the trouble of doing so. So there was no need of hesitation, and in the next moment we were out for a walk on a country road.

At first we were speechless. She appeared to me no longer approachable with the familiarity of "Tomo-chan." But as the autumnal breeze cooled down her bashfulness, and the beauty of the scenery was absorbing her attention more and more, I ventured to falter:

"Tomo-chan!"

"Yes?"

She looked at me with her eyes beaming with laughter, and there was the same old innocent childhood, but where was the bashfulness?

"Do you find this beautiful?" I asked.

"Yes, certainly."

"It wasn't so beautiful yesterday."

"You mean to say that you had a sudden frost last night that tinged the leaves?" she archly asked.

"Why, more sudden than that; it got to be lovelier this very afternoon. We've had something better than a frost."

"How is it possible?" She laughed.

"No stranger than that you are changed so *beautifully* in a year."

I said what I should not have said, for she blushed to the roots of her hair, and I repented of my forwardness.

"But come along, Tomo-chan. I'll show you what you have not seen yet."

And I took her over the hill and pointed to the faint shadow of the peerless mountain.

"Why, Fujiyama!" she exclaimed. "Oh, how lovely! Could you see that every day from here?"

"Not in rainy weather. . . . But she wanted to see you to-day, as everybody else did, and waited there from morning."

"I wish you would thank her for that, Sakae-san."

"You ought first to thank him who told her about your coming."

"Oh," she smilingly said, "but don't tell me his name now, as I want to repay him afterwards — abundantly."

I touched her dimple as she said so, and then we went to the secluded part of the hill where the crimson branches of maples were projecting from the green back ground, the red frosted "crows' melons" festooned high on the criptomerias, and the wild chrysanthemums were blooming lavishly. In such a charming spot Tomo-chan was a child of thirteen, and wanted me to take "crows' melons" — I wonder if she remembered the watermelon incident? — and to gather chrysanthemums, and laughed and sang to her heart's content. She was her old very self. As the setting sun was resting on her shoulder, I decked her hair with wild flowers, and whispered in her ear that she would remember evermore the day we spent together. She nodded, and smiled the sweetest of smiles.

THE END.

Sakae Shioya in 1955.

Sakae Shioya (1873–1961) attended Tokyo's First Imperial College and came to the United States in 1901. He earned an M.A. degree from the University of Chicago in 1903 and a Ph.D. from Yale University in 1906, both in English. He published English translations of works by contemporary Japanese writers, including Rohan Koda and Kenjiro Tokutomi. In addition to this childhood memoir, his later works included *Chushingura: An Exposition* (1940).

www.ingramcontent.com/pod-product-compliance
Lightning Source LLC
Chambersburg PA
CBHW032144040426
42449CB00005B/401